PRE-WORK
FOR

THE GOOD $ENSE
BUDGET COURSE

IMPORTANT

Please read and complete all pre-work prior to attending the course.

Dear Good $ense Budget Course Participant,

We're glad you're registered for the *Good $ense Budget Course*! Regardless of your financial situation, a budget—what we call a "Spending Plan"—is the necessary and fundamental tool that enables you to control your money rather than having your money control you. Contrary to popular thought, a Spending Plan is not restrictive; rather, it is freeing. We believe the *Good $ense Budget Course* will prove this truth to you.

Course Goal

The goal of the *Good $ense Budget Course* is for you to commit to and begin developing a biblically-based Spending Plan. By the end of the course, you will have a Spending Plan in your hand, the knowledge in your head to implement it, and a commitment in your heart to follow through on it. The commitment of the Good $ense Ministry is to provide you with the principles, practical steps, and individual assistance to help make that happen.

Pre-work

In order for the course to be as valuable and productive as possible, it is very important to complete the pre-work prior to attending the course. Completing the forms may take several hours so it is advisable to begin as soon as your receive these materials. The information you are asked to collect is confidential and no one else will see it. Throughout the course, you will use your pre-work information to establish your personal Spending Plan.

Supplies

In addition to your completed pre-work, please bring to the course two or three pencils, an eraser, and a pocket calculator.

Prayer

Pray that this experience will be a valuable one for you and the others in attendance, and that we will all grow in our understanding of Biblical Financial Principles and our ability to put them into practice.

Looking forward to seeing you there!

The Good $ense Ministry

PRE-WORK INSTRUCTIONS

Six forms are included in the pre-work to help you prepare for the *Good $ense Budget Course.* Please allow plenty of time prior to attending the course to gather the information and to complete each form. Instructions to help you complete each form are listed below.

Goals to Achieve this Year

Make it a priority to reflect on your financial goals. If you are married, make time to discuss financial goals with your spouse. These goals will become the basis for shaping your Spending Plan, and they will provide motivation for following through on your decisions in the months ahead.

What I Owe

As you fill out the second column (Amount) of this section, use the total balance due on each item.

What I Own

These sections are optional, but we encourage you to fill them out so you can calculate a simplified version of your "net worth." Consider that the value of things you own should be the amount you would expect to get if you sold the items.

Gift List

Here's an often overlooked or underestimated part of spending. Write the names of individuals you will be purchasing gifts for in the coming year. Remember to include cards, postage at Christmas, parties, etc. You may wish to include some money for as yet unannounced weddings, etc.

What I Spend

Gather as much information as you can to determine a monthly average for expenses in each category. Going through your checkbook and your credit card bills for the past year will probably be helpful. Be sure to include periodic expense items such as auto insurance, taxes, etc., that may not be paid on a monthly basis. If you have not kept records in the past, some of the categories may be difficult to estimate. Give it your best shot, recognizing that if you don't have records showing how much you're spending in a particular area, the amount is probably more than you think it is!

The Income figures at the top of the page should be your take-home pay after taxes and other deductions. Make a note of any deductions (such as medical insurance, retirement, etc.). Where those items occur under expenses, enter the notation "payroll deduction." If your income varies from month to month, use a conservative monthly estimate based on the last two or three years' earnings. Referring back to your income tax records could be helpful in making this determination. Remember, you are looking for after-tax, take-home income.

Money Motivation Quiz

This is an optional exercise that will provide insightful information on your behavior regarding money. If you are married, two copies of the quiz are provided so you and your spouse can both take the quiz. Answers are included on the back of the quiz. No fair peeking before you answer the questions!

GOALS TO ACHIEVE THIS YEAR

Please allow adequate time to give serious consideration to your goals. Carefully considered, realistic goals—that flow out of what's really important to you—are powerful motivators. That motivation will be very helpful to you in following through on the steps necessary to achieve your goals.

OVERALL GOAL

My overall goal in attending this course is:

_____

_____

SPECIFIC GOALS TO ACHIEVE

Check the appropriate boxes and write in any details on the lines to the right of each item.

❏ Pay off debt: _____

❏ Save for a major purchase (home, car, other): _____

❏ Save for a dream vacation: _____

❏ Save for emergencies: _____

❏ Save to replace items that may wear out (major appliances, home repairs, car): _____

❏ Save for college expenses: _____

❏ Save for retirement: _____

❏ Increase my giving to the church: _____

❏ Increase other giving: _____

❏ Other: _____

❏ Other: _____

❏ Other: _____

What I Own (optional)

I Own (assets)	Amount
Checking Account	
Savings Account	
Other Savings	
Insurance (cash value)	
Retirement	
Home (market value)	
Auto (market value)	
Second Auto (market value)	
Other Possessions (estimate)	
Money Owed to Me	
Other	
Other	
Total of All I Own	

What I Owe

I Owe (liabilities)	Amount	Minimum Monthly Payment	Interest Percentage
Mortgage (current balance)			
Home Equity Loans			
Credit Cards			
Car Loans			
Education Loans			
Family/Friends			
Other			
Total of All I Owe			

Net Worth (optional)
(Total of All I Own – Total of All I owe = Net Worth (in earthly terms, not God's!)*

_____ – _____ = _____

*Never confuse your self-worth with your net worth. In God's eyes each one of us is of infinite worth.

GIFT LIST

List the names of those you for whom you buy gifts and the amounts you typically spend on each occasion.*

Name	Birthday	Christmas	Anniversary	Other
1.				
2.				
3.				
4.				
5.				
6.				
7.				
8.				
9.				
10.				
11.				
12.				
13.				
14.				
15.				
16.				
17.				
18.				
19.				
20.				
Total				

GRAND TOTAL $_____   MONTHLY AVERAGE (Total ÷ 12) = $_____
(of all columns)

*You may wish to also include the cost of holiday decorations, entertaining, etc.

What I Spend

EARNINGS/INCOME PER MONTH	TOTALS
Salary #1 (net take-home)	_____
Salary #2 (net take-home)	_____
Other (less taxes)	_____
TOTAL MONTHLY INCOME	$_____

% GUIDE

1. GIVING $_____

Church	_____
OTHER CONTRIBUTIONS	_____

2. SAVING   5–10% $_____

EMERGENCY	_____
REPLACEMENT	_____
LONG TERM	_____

3. DEBT   0–10% $_____

CREDIT CARDS:	
VISA	_____
Master Card	_____
Discover	_____
American Express	_____
Gas Cards	_____
Department Stores	_____
EDUCATION LOANS	_____
OTHER LOANS:	
Bank Loans	_____
Credit Union	_____
Family/Friends	_____
Other	_____

4. HOUSING   25–38% $_____

MORTGAGE/TAXES/RENT	_____
MAINTENANCE/REPAIRS	_____
UTILITIES:	
Electric	_____
Gas	_____
Water	_____
Trash	_____
Telephone/Internet	_____
Cable TV	_____
Other	_____

5. AUTO/TRANSP.   12–15% $_____

CAR PAYMENTS/LICENSE	_____
GAS & BUS/TRAIN/PARKING	_____
OIL/LUBE/MAINTENANCE	_____

6. INSURANCE
(Paid by you)   5% $_____

AUTO	_____
HOMEOWNERS	_____
LIFE	_____
MEDICAL/DENTAL	_____
Other	_____

7. HOUSEHOLD/PERSONAL   15–25% $_____

GROCERIES	_____
CLOTHES/DRY CLEANING	_____
GIFTS	_____
HOUSEHOLD ITEMS	_____
PERSONAL:	
Liquor/Tobacco	_____
Cosmetics	_____
Barber/Beauty	_____
OTHER:	
Books/Magazines	_____
Allowances	_____
Music Lessons	_____
Personal Technology	_____
Education	_____
Miscellaneous	_____

8. ENTERTAINMENT   5–10% $_____

GOING OUT:	
Meals	_____
Movies/Events	_____
Baby-sitting	_____
TRAVEL (VACATION/TRIPS)	_____
OTHER:	
Fitness/Sports	_____
Hobbies	_____
Media Rental	_____
Other	_____

9. PROF. SERVICES   5–15% $_____

CHILD CARE	_____
MEDICAL/DENTAL/PRESC.	_____
OTHER	
Legal	_____
Counseling	_____
Professional Dues	_____

10. MISC. SMALL CASH EXPENDITURES   2-3% $_____

TOTAL EXPENSES $_____

TOTAL MONTHLY INCOME	$_____
LESS TOTAL EXPENSES	$_____
INCOME OVER/(UNDER) EXPENSES	$_____

* This is a % of total monthly income. These are guidelines only and may be different for individual situations. However, there should be good rationale for a significant variance.

MONEY MOTIVATION QUIZ

Directions

For each of the fourteen questions below, circle the letter that best describes your response.

1. Money is important because it allows me to . . .
   a. Do what I want to do.
   b. Feel secure.
   c. Get ahead in life.
   d. Buy things for others.

2. I feel that money . . .
   a. Frees up my time.
   b. Can solve my problems.
   c. Is a means to an end.
   d. Helps make relationships smoother.

3. When it comes to saving money, I . . .
   a. Don't have a plan and rarely save.
   b. Have a plan and stick to it.
   c. Don't have a plan but manage to save anyway.
   d. Don't make enough money to save.

4. If someone asks about my personal finances, I . . .
   a. Feel defensive.
   b. Realize I need more education and information.
   c. Feel comfortable and competent.
   d. Would rather talk about something else.

5. When I make a major purchase, I . . .
   a. Go with what my intuition tells me.
   b. Research a great deal before buying.
   c. Feel I'm in charge—it's my/our money.
   d. Ask friends/family first.

6. If I have money left over at the end of the month, I . . .
   a. Go out and have a good time.
   b. Put the money into savings.
   c. Look for a good investment.
   d. Buy a gift for someone.

7. If I discover I paid more for something than a friend did I . . .
   a. Couldn't care less.
   b. Feel it's okay because I also find bargains at times.
   c. Assume they spent more time shopping, and time is money.
   d. Feel upset and angry at myself.

8. When paying bills, I . . .
   a. Put it off and sometimes forget.
   b. Pay them when due, but no sooner.
   c. Pay when I get to it, but don't want to be hassled.
   d. Worry that my credit will suffer if I miss a payment.

9. When it comes to borrowing money I . . .
   a. Simply won't/don't like to feel indebted.
   b. Only borrow as a last resort.
   c. Tend to borrow from banks or other business sources.
   d. Ask friends and family because they know I'll pay.

10. When eating out with friends I prefer to . . .
    a. Divide the bill proportionately.
    b. Ask for separate checks.
    c. Charge the bill to my bankcard and have others pay me.
    d. Pay the entire bill because I like to treat my friends.

11. When it comes to tipping I . . .
    a. Sometimes do and sometimes don't.
    b. Just call me Scrooge.
    c. Resent it, but always tip the right amount.
    d. Tip generously because I like to be well thought of.

12. If I suddenly came into a lot of money, I . . .
    a. Wouldn't have to work.
    b. Wouldn't have to worry about the future.
    c. Could really build up my business.
    d. Would spend a lot on family and friends and enjoy time with them more.

13. When indecisive about a purchase I often tell myself . . .
    a. It's only money.
    b. It's a bargain.
    c. It's a good investment.
    d. He/she will love it.

14. In our family . . .
    a. I do/will handle all the money and pay all the bills.
    b. My partner does/will take care of the finances.
    c. I do/will pay my bills and my partner will do the same.
    d. We do/will sit down together to pay bills.

15. Bonus question: Describe how money was handled in your family of origin. Who managed the family budget? Was that person a spender or a saver? Which are you?

Score: Tally your answers to questions one through fourteen by the letter of your answer:

a. _____   c. _____
b. _____   d. _____

To understand your results, see the explanation on the back of this page.

UNDERSTANDING THE RESULTS OF YOUR MONEY MOTIVATION QUIZ

Money means different things to different people based on a variety of factors such as temperament and life experiences. Often the meaning of money and the way it motivates us is subtle and something we are not always aware of.

This simple quiz is designed to give you an indication of how strongly you are influenced by the following money motivations: Freedom, Security, Power, and Love. None are inherently good or bad, although each certainly has its dark side.

The key to your money motivation is reflected in the relative number of a, b, c, or d answers.

"A" answers indicate that money relates to **Freedom**. To you money means having the freedom to do what you like.

"B" answers indicate that money relates to **Security**. You need to feel safe and secure and you desire the stability and protection that money supposedly provides.

"C" answers indicate that money relates to **Power**. Personal success and control are important to you, and you appreciate the power money sometimes provides.

"D" answers indicate that money relates to **Love**. You like to use money to express love and build relationships.

One of the keys to managing money wisely is to understand our relationship to it. We hope this exercise gives you some helpful insights. You may wish to share your scores with your spouse or a friend and discuss whether their perceptions of your money motivations are consistent with your scores.

MONEY MOTIVATION QUIZ

Directions

For each of the fourteen questions below, circle the letter that best describes your response.

1. Money is important because it allows me to . . .
   a. Do what I want to do.
   b. Feel secure.
   c. Get ahead in life.
   d. Buy things for others.

2. I feel that money . . .
   a. Frees up my time.
   b. Can solve my problems.
   c. Is a means to an end.
   d. Helps make relationships smoother.

3. When it comes to saving money, I . . .
   a. Don't have a plan and rarely save.
   b. Have a plan and stick to it.
   c. Don't have a plan but manage to save anyway.
   d. Don't make enough money to save.

4. If someone asks about my personal finances, I . . .
   a. Feel defensive.
   b. Realize I need more education and information.
   c. Feel comfortable and competent.
   d. Would rather talk about something else.

5. When I make a major purchase, I . . .
   a. Go with what my intuition tells me.
   b. Research a great deal before buying.
   c. Feel I'm in charge—it's my/our money.
   d. Ask friends/family first.

6. If I have money left over at the end of the month, I . . .
   a. Go out and have a good time.
   b. Put the money into savings.
   c. Look for a good investment.
   d. Buy a gift for someone.

7. If I discover I paid more for something than a friend did I . . .
   a. Couldn't care less.
   b. Feel it's okay because I also find bargains at times.
   c. Assume they spent more time shopping, and time is money.
   d. Feel upset and angry at myself.

8. When paying bills, I . . .
   a. Put it off and sometimes forget.
   b. Pay them when due, but no sooner.
   c. Pay when I get to it, but don't want to be hassled.
   d. Worry that my credit will suffer if I miss a payment.

9. When it comes to borrowing money I . . .
   a. Simply won't/don't like to feel indebted.
   b. Only borrow as a last resort.
   c. Tend to borrow from banks or other business sources.
   d. Ask friends and family because they know I'll pay.

10. When eating out with friends I prefer to . . .
    a. Divide the bill proportionately.
    b. Ask for separate checks.
    c. Charge the bill to my bankcard and have others pay me.
    d. Pay the entire bill because I like to treat my friends.

11. When it comes to tipping I . . .
    a. Sometimes do and sometimes don't.
    b. Just call me Scrooge.
    c. Resent it, but always tip the right amount.
    d. Tip generously because I like to be well thought of.

12. If I suddenly came into a lot of money, I . . .
    a. Wouldn't have to work.
    b. Wouldn't have to worry about the future.
    c. Could really build up my business.
    d. Would spend a lot on family and friends and enjoy time with them more.

13. When indecisive about a purchase I often tell myself . . .
    a. It's only money.
    b. It's a bargain.
    c. It's a good investment.
    d. He/she will love it.

14. In our family . . .
    a. I do/will handle all the money and pay all the bills.
    b. My partner does/will take care of the finances.
    c. I do/will pay my bills and my partner will do the same.
    d. We do/will sit down together to pay bills.

15. Bonus question: Describe how money was handled in your family of origin. Who managed the family budget? Was that person a spender or a saver? Which are you?

Score: Tally your answers to questions one through fourteen by the letter of your answer:

a. _____ c. _____
b. _____ d. _____

To understand your results, see the explanation on the back of this page.

UNDERSTANDING THE RESULTS OF YOUR MONEY MOTIVATION QUIZ

Money means different things to different people based on a variety of factors such as temperament and life experiences. Often the meaning of money and the way it motivates us is subtle and something we are not always aware of.

This simple quiz is designed to give you an indication of how strongly you are influenced by the following money motivations: Freedom, Security, Power, and Love. None are inherently good or bad, although each certainly has its dark side.

The key to your money motivation is reflected in the relative number of a, b, c, or d answers.

"A" answers indicate that money relates to **Freedom**. To you money means having the freedom to do what you like.

"B" answers indicate that money relates to **Security**. You need to feel safe and secure and you desire the stability and protection that money supposedly provides.

"C" answers indicate that money relates to **Power**. Personal success and control are important to you, and you appreciate the power money sometimes provides.

"D" answers indicate that money relates to **Love**. You like to use money to express love and build relationships.

One of the keys to managing money wisely is to understand our relationship to it. We hope this exercise gives you some helpful insights. You may wish to share your scores with your spouse or a friend and discuss whether their perceptions of your money motivations are consistent with your scores.

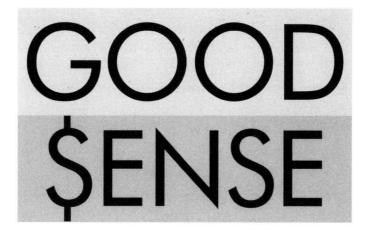

BUDGET COURSE

Biblical Financial Principles for
Transforming Your Finances and Life

GOOD $ENSE

BUDGET COURSE

Biblical Financial Principles for
Transforming Your Finances and Life

Participant's Guide

**Dick Towner
and John Tofilon**

With contributions from
the Good $ense Ministry team of
Willow Creek Community Church

WILLOW CREEK
RESOURCES

ZONDERVAN™

GRAND RAPIDS, MICHIGAN 49530

Good $ense Budget Course Participant's Guide
Copyright © 2002 by Willow Creek Community Church

Requests for information should be addressed to:

Willow Creek Association
67 E. Algonquin Road
Barrington, IL 60010

Zondervan
5300 Patterson SE
Grand Rapids, MI 49530

ISBN: 0-744-13728-4

Cover design by Rick Devon, Adam Beasley

Interior design by Ann Gjeldum

Produced with the assistance of the Livingstone Corporation. Project staff includes: Ashley Taylor, Christopher D. Hudson, Carol Barnstable, and Paige Drygas.

Printed in the United States of America

04 05 06 07/ / 10 9 8 7 6 5 4

DEDICATION

Dick Towner:

To Pop and Gram Wernicke who raised me and modeled for me a simple and frugal lifestyle. While their lifestyle was shaped in part by income circumstances, it was lived with contentment, making it easy for me to later accept the biblical truth that a person's life does not consist in the abundance of their possessions.

To my incredibly gifted and incredibly loving wife, Sibyl, who helped me to understand that frugality for its own sake simply leads to sinful hoarding, but that the true end result of frugality is liberality. Thank you, dear Sibyl, for modeling this for me and for helping me to experience the joy of giving.

And finally, to the body of believers known as College Hill Presbyterian Church in Cincinnati, Ohio. Not only did you baptize me as a child, nurture me as a teenager, marry me as a young adult, mature my faith, ordain me as an elder, and allow me to serve as part of the ministerial team for fourteen years, but you encouraged and provided the platform for the development of the vast majority of what is contained within these pages. My gratitude is beyond expression.

John Tofilon:

There is nothing like getting involved in what God is doing, especially when the tug of the Holy Spirit turns into a lifelong calling. This project is dedicated to the following people whose influence has enabled me to fulfill that calling.

To Bruce Saarela, for giving me the opportunity over twenty years ago to develop my skills and passion by designing and teaching budget seminars. To Kent Carlson, for making "the ask" ten years later to get back in the game. To Dick Towner, for leaving the door wide open for me to be creative, sometimes at the cost of his sanity. To

Bill Hybels, for challenging me to lean into my calling. To my wife, Charlotte, for thirty years of being my support; and to our three children—David, Christopher, Kaitlin—for enduring my budget mantras. To the Lord for showing me the need, giving me the vision, and sustaining me through it all.

Finally, this project is dedicated to you, the reader and course participant. I hope and pray this course helps you on your journey in becoming the person God wants you to be.

CONTENTS

FOREWORD

In school they tell us we're being equipped to earn it. Then for the rest of our lives—for about fifty or sixty hours a week—we're busy making it. We invest countless hours in thought and discussion deciding how to deal with it. We walk around shopping malls for hours on end determining how we're going to spend it. We're caught up more often than we'd like to admit worrying we won't have enough of it. We dream and scheme to figure out ways to acquire more of it.

Arguments over it are a leading cause for marital disintegration. Despair over losing it has even led to suicide. Passion for it causes much of society's crime. The absence of it causes many of society's nightmares. Some view it as the root of all evil, while others think of it as the means for great good.

One thing is clear: We cannot afford to ignore the reality of the importance of *money.*

Over the years at Willow Creek Community Church we've been committed to tackling every important issue that faces the people who attend—from nutrition to sexuality, from building character to deepening relationships, from discovering and adoring the identity of God to preparing for death and eternity. One topic, however, that we've learned we must address regularly and directly is the subject that Christians wrestle with almost every day—the issue of how we handle personal finances.

Thankfully, there's no shortage of information on this crucial matter in the Bible, and it provides the basis for the materials you're about to dive into. More than two thousand Scripture passages touch on the theme of money. Jesus spoke about it frequently. About two-thirds of Jesus' parables make reference to our use of financial resources. He once warned that "where your treasure is, there your heart will be also." He talked often about these matters because he understood what was at stake. He knew that, left to our own devices, this area would quickly become a source of pain and frustration—and sometimes bondage. Worse, he saw how easily our hearts would be led astray from pure devotion to God into areas of worry and even obsession over possessions. He wanted to protect us from these pitfalls and to show us the liberty that comes from following him fully in every area of life, including this one.

So get ready to join the ranks of thousands of people from our church and other churches who have received tangible help in this area through Good $ense. This vital ministry has been refined and proven over many years by my friend and trusted co-laborer, Dick Towner, along with his Good $ense Ministry team. I'm confident you'll find fresh avenues to increased financial freedom and, along the way, grow a more grateful spirit and generous heart.

And as you and others from your congregation experience this, your church will be liberated so it can reflect more and more of that giving spirit and heart to the community around you, making it a magnet to people who are desperately looking for the kind of freedom, life, and love they see in you.

Bill Hybels
Founding and Senior Pastor
Willow Creek Community Church

ACKNOWLEDGMENTS

There are literally hundreds of people at Willow Creek Community Church and the Willow Creek Association whose expertise, support, wide array of contributions and encouragement were crucial throughout the development and completion of this project. Though space limitations prohibit naming all of them, their ranks include the following:

- The early group of volunteers and staff member George Lindholm who responded to God's vision in 1985 and began the Good $ense Ministry. Their leadership ranks included Warren Beach, Bill and Loretta Gaunt, John Frederick, Chuck Keenon, Jim Kinney, and Carl Tielsch. Stalwarts of the early counseling team included Bill and Joann Allen, Bob Baker, Candy Borst, Barry Gardner, Don and Zona Hackman, Dan Hollerick, Charlie Maxwell, Elizabeth Maring, Tom Stevens, Cyndy Sutherland, and Carol White. Staff assistance in the early years also came from Bruce Bugbee and Ken Fillipini.

- Current Good $ense volunteers, especially the following who have played an active role in the development of the materials: Russ Haan, Jerry Wiseman, Steve Sherbondy, Jenifer Nordeen-Lugar, Dan Rotter and Sue Drake. Thank you for your creativity and passion and the many contributions you made. Thanks, too, to the volunteer Good $ense Ministry Board, not only for your wise counsel and direction over the years, but even more for the deep bonds of friendship and mutual call to ministry we have shared.

- Norm Vander Wel and Jon Kopke, two friends of the heart who, though not connected with Willow Creek, provided insight and creativity and encouragement that was exceedingly helpful.

- Jim Riley, who followed me as director of the Good $ense Ministry at Willow Creek Community Church, and has been a true companion of the heart in seeking to help folks understand and implement biblical principles of stewardship in their lives. Thank you, Jim, for your commitment to this project and for your deep friendship.

- Wendy Seidman and her team—Bridget Purdome, Sue Drake, and Rebecca Adler. Their expertise in instructional design makes these materials effective in training and equipping people. Thanks to each of you not only for sharing your expertise but for taking the core values of this project into your own hearts.

- Christine M. Anderson, who managed the project, interjected her insights and wisdom at all the right times, provided encouragement when it was most needed, and exhibited amazing patience as we worked and reworked and reworked the material.

- Bob Gustafson, Steve Pederson, and Sharon Sherbondy for their expertise and enthusiasm in creating video segments that not only teach and train but also touch the heart.

- Bill Hybels, senior pastor. Early in his ministry Bill recognized and affirmed the vital connection between a biblical understanding of material possessions and ones spiritual well being. Over the years, his commitment to regular, passionate teaching on this topic has been an invaluable support and encouragement to the Good $ense Ministry . . . and a significant contribution to its effectiveness.

- Jim Mellado, Sharon Swing, and the entire Willow Creek Association Leadership Team for catching the vision for this project and for their support and encouragement as we worked to realize that vision.

- Joe Sherman and the publishing and marketing team at the Willow Creek Association for providing the resources to produce this curriculum and for believing it can make a difference is so many lives.

- Several donors whose faith in this project and generous financial contributions not only provided initial funding but were also a great encouragement to me personally.

OUR HOPES FOR YOU

Dear Participant:

We are so glad you've decided to attend the *Good $ense Budget Course!* Although we don't know what your financial situation is or what motivated you to sign up for the course, we do have deeply held hopes for you.

We hope the *Good $ense Budget Course* will be more than just a learning experience about budgets, finances, and your relationship to money. We hope it will also be a time for you to reflect on your relationship to God. This often happens naturally because our relationship to money is closely correlated to our relationship to God.

We hope you leave the course more aware of how your financial behavior is influenced—many times subconsciously—by forces within our culture that may or may not be consistent with your values and goals.

We hope you will discover tools and develop skills that will enable you to manage and control your finances, rather than allowing your finances to manage and control you. Money is a powerful thing. If we fail to control it, it will make many key life decisions for us—where we live, what jobs we take, who our friends are, and more. We want you to gain the skills to really master your money so you can experience a freedom in Christ you may have never known before.

Finally, we hope you leave this course with a deep sense of confidence that—with God's help—you really can do it! We want you to leave with a budget in your hand, the knowledge in your head to implement it, and the desire and motivation in your heart to follow through on it.

We hope and pray that all these will be true for you.

Dick Towner and John Tofilon

THE FINANCIAL DILEMMA

WELCOME TO THE GOOD $ENSE BUDGET COURSE!

Objectives

In this session, you will:

1. Discover three prominent cultural myths about money.

2. Identify which cultural myth influences you most.

3. Reflect on how being a "trustee" versus an "owner" affects you.

4. Discover what a Spending Plan is and what its benefits are.

Introduction and Welcome

You can do it!

> Philippians 4:13: "*I can do everything through him who gives me strength.*"

"Money is a powerful thing!"

The Pull of the Culture

Most of us find ourselves in one of four financial situations:

- Crisis

- One paycheck from disaster

- Good "financial" shape

- God-honoring lifestyle

Money is the chief rival god.

If we don't control our money, it will control us:

- where we live

- where we work

- who we have as friends

- how we use our time

Video: *The Pull of the Culture*

Use the space provided to write any notes.

> **Notes**

Cultural Myths

- "Things bring happiness."

- "Debt is _____ and unavoidable."

- "A little more money will solve all your problems."

Group Activity: *The Pull of the Culture*

1. Form a group with two or three other people.

2. Introduce yourself to each other.

3. Share with your group the cultural myth that influences you most and how it impacts you.

Notes

Course Overview

- Contrast what the culture says about money with what the Bible says about money.

- Develop personal Spending Plans.

Matthew 6:21: *"Where your treasure is, there your heart will be also."*

Every financial decision is also a *spiritual* decision.

The Mind and Heart of God

Three Truths:

- God created everything (Genesis 1:1).

- God owns everything.

> Psalm 50: *"Every animal of the forest is mine, and the cattle on a thousand hills . . . for the world is mine and all that is in it."*
>
> Psalm 24:1: *"The earth is the LORD's and everything in it, the world, and all who live in it."*

- We are trustees.

> 1 Corinthians 4:2: *"Now it is required that those who have been given a trust must prove faithful."*

  ○ A trustee has no rights, only responsibilities.

  ○ In eternal terms, _____ we possess belongs to God.

Video: *The Pearl of Great Price*

Notes

Group Activity: *Discussion of The Pearl of Great Price*

1. Get back into your groups.

2. Discuss your reaction to the video and how this truth might impact you.

Notes

The Pull of the Culture vs. the Mind and Heart of God

FOOLISH   FAITHFUL

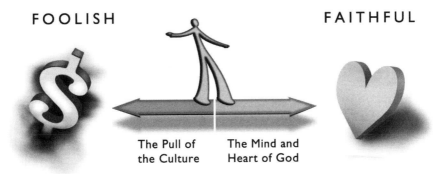

The Pull of   The Mind and
the Culture   Heart of God

The Financial Dilemma

- One servant
- Two masters

> Matthew 6:24 (NLT): *"No one can serve two masters. For you will hate one and love the other, or be devoted to one and despise the other. You cannot serve both God and money."*

> Matthew 6:33: *"Seek first his kingdom and his righteousness, and all these things will be given to you as well."*

> Matthew 25: *". . . good and faithful servants."*

> Luke 12:21 (NLT): *"Yes, a person is a fool to store up earthly wealth but not have a rich relationship with God."*

Two Great Truths:

- God holds us _____ for how we manage the money and possessions entrusted to us.

- We will be found either faithful or foolish.

 Key Question: Will God consider my financial decisions to be faithful or foolish?

Five Financial Areas

- Earning

- Giving

- Saving

- Debt

- Spending

When we choose to be faithful in these five financial areas, Scripture indicates that we become a:

- Diligent Earner

- _____ Giver

- Wise Saver

- _____ Debtor

- Prudent Consumer

Genuine financial freedom is:

The _____ we experience as we faithfully manage our financial resources according to God's purposes and principles.

Being financially faithful leads to being financially free!

The Spending Plan

What Is a Spending Plan?

A budget is . . .

- The fundamental tool that enables us to control our money so that it doesn't end up controlling us.

- A Spending Plan for how we will allocate our financial resources.

A Spending Plan is:

- A way to reach our financial _____ and live out our values and priorities.

A Spending Plan:

- Produces _____.

    There is no true freedom without limits.

- Sets safe limits financially.

The Benefits of a Spending Plan

❏ Gives us facts.

❏ Avoids _____.

❏ Keeps our _____ and priorities in check.

❏ Leads to financial freedom.

A Spending Plan is for *everyone*—not just those in financial difficulty.

SESSION SUMMARY

Course Goal

Commit to and begin developing a biblically-based Spending Plan.

Course Objectives

- Become aware of the Pull of the Culture

- Understand Biblical Financial Principles

- Develop a first draft of a Spending Plan

- Select a record-keeping system

- Commit to implementing the Spending Plan and record-keeping system

Course Sessions

- Session 1: The Financial Dilemma

- Session 2: Earning, Giving, and Saving

- Session 3: Saving and Debt

- Session 4: Spending

- Session 5: Balancing the Spending Plan

- Session 6: Record Keeping and Commitment

EARNING, GIVING, AND SAVING

OBJECTIVES

In this session, you will:

1. Prioritize your financial goals.

2. Reflect on how you can become closer to the Mind and Heart of God as an earner, a giver, and a saver.

3. Complete the Spending Plan worksheet for income and giving.

Individual Activity: *Goals to Achieve This Year*

In light of what we covered in the previous session, review your pre-work sheet to determine if you want to keep your goals the same or make any changes. If you were not able to complete this portion of the pre-work, do so now.

Prioritize your goals, and list the top three in the space provided:

Goal 1: _____

Goal 2: _____

Goal 3: _____

Earning

The Pull of the Culture vs. the Mind and Heart of God

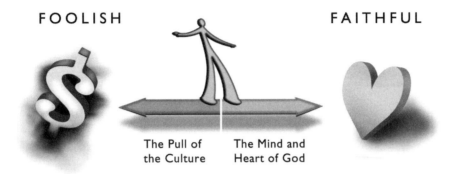

FOOLISH   FAITHFUL

The Pull of the Culture   The Mind and Heart of God

The Pull of the Culture on the earner says:

- "Your value is measured by your _____ and your paycheck."

- "A little more money will solve all your problems."

The Mind and Heart of God counters:

- Our value is not measured by what we do but by who we are—beloved sons and daughters of God.

- We are called to join him in the ongoing management of his creation.

- Work is a _____, not a curse.

The Diligent Earner is:

One who works with commitment, purpose, and a grateful attitude.

- Be diligent.

> Colossians 3:23 (NLT): *"Work hard and cheerfully at whatever you do."*

- Be _____.

> Colossians 3:23 (NLT): *"[Work] as though you were working for the Lord rather than for people."*

  ○ Serve God.

  ○ Provide for ourselves and those dependent on us.

> 1 Timothy 5:8 (NLT): *"Those who won't care for their own relatives . . . have denied what we believe."*

- Be _____.

> Deuteronomy 8:17-18: *"You may say to yourself, 'My power and the strength of my hands have produced this wealth for me.' Remember the LORD your God, for it is he who gives you the ability to produce wealth."*

Practical Tips on Earning

Net take-home pay is:

The amount of the paycheck *after* all _____ and deductions.

Variable Income:

Take a _____ estimate of your after-tax annual income (based on your income of the past few years) and divide by twelve.

Example: $30,000 ÷ 12 = $2,500 per month*

Two-Income Strategy:

Cover all the basics—all ongoing necessary expenses—with one income. For example:

- Giving
- Savings
- Housing
- Food
- Clothing
- Transportation
- Basic household
- Basic entertainment

*See page 107 in the Appendix for more information.

The second income should be used only for "extras":

- Additional giving

- Additional savings

- Accelerated debt repayment

- Additional travel and entertainment

- Other non-essentials

All these items should be paid with cash.

If your present situation makes it impossible to meet basic expenses with one income, then put a significant amount of that second income into savings so that there is money in reserve in case that second income is lost.

Question: What happens to your raises?

(See page 108 in the Appendix.)

Deciding _____ how you'll use raises is a key strategy in reaching your financial goals.

Individual Activity: *Spending Plan Application*

Fill in the Income category on the Spending Plan worksheet.

Giving

Video: *The Offering*

Notes

The Pull of the Culture vs. the Mind and Heart of God

FOOLISH   FAITHFUL

The Pull of   The Mind and
the Culture   Heart of God

Three Myths:

- "Give if it _____ you."

- "Give if there is anything left over."

- "Give out of a sense of duty."

The Generous Giver is:

One who gives with an obedient will, a joyful attitude, and a compassionate heart.

- We are made to give.

- Why God wants us to give:

  ○ As a response to God's _____.

  > James 1:17 (NLT): *"Whatever is good and perfect comes to us from God above."*

  ○ To focus on him as our source of security

  > Matthew 6:19-20a (NLT): *"Don't store up treasures here on earth, where they can be eaten by moths, and get rusty, and where thieves break in and steal. Store your treasures in heaven."*

  > Matthew 6:32b-33 (NLT): *"Your heavenly Father already knows all your needs, and he will give you all you need from day to day if you live for him and make the kingdom of God your primary concern."*

  ○ To help achieve economic justice

  ○ To bless others and to be blessed

  ○ To break the _____ of money

Individual Activity: *The Generous Giver*

1. After thinking through the Mind and Heart of God on giving, in what way is God nudging you?

2. Is there an action step he wants you to take? If so, write it in the space provided.

Practical Tips on Giving

The biblical benchmark for giving is the tithe.

For those not at the tithe:

- Develop a _____ to reach the tithe.

- Begin by giving _____.

For those at the tithe:

The tithe is a wonderful goal to aspire to; it's a terrible place to stop.

 Key Question: How much of God's money do I need to live on?

Individual Activity: *Spending Plan Application*

1. Refer back to page 30 where your goals are listed, and page 37 where your action step for giving is written. Consider your current financial situation and what you are becoming as a giver.

2. Set a short-term goal for giving, and fill in the giving line on your Spending Plan worksheet.

Saving

The Pull of the Culture vs. the Mind and Heart of God

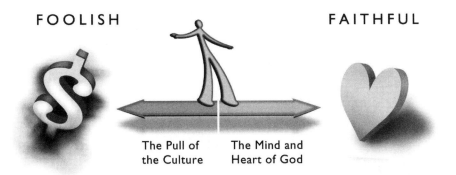

FOOLISH   FAITHFUL

The Pull of   The Mind and
the Culture   Heart of God

Two Cultural Myths:

- "If you have it, _____ it; and if you don't have it, spend it anyway."

- "It is futile to save."

The Wise Saver is:

One who builds, preserves, and invests with discernment.

The Mind and Heart of God on saving is:

- It is wise to save.

> Proverbs 21:20: *"In the house of the wise are stores of choice food and oil, . . . but the foolish . . . devour all [they have]."*

- It is sinful to hoard. (Luke 12:16-21)

What's the difference between saving and hoarding?

- Saving is putting money aside for _____ goals.

- Hoarding is continuing to put money aside after our goals are reached.

How can we avoid hoarding?

- Understand our _____

- Answer the question, "When is enough, enough?"

> Ecclesiastes 5:10 (NLT): *"Those who love money will never have enough."*

Group Activity: *Your Money Tendency*

1. Check the box below that applies to you. If you completed the Money Motivation Quiz in the pre-work, you can use those results instead.

   Money is important to me because it allows me:

   ❏ *Freedom—to do what I want to do. Independence is important to me. Money means having the freedom to do what I want.*

   ❏ *Security—to feel safe. Stability is important to me. Money means having protection from life's uncertainties.*

   ❏ *Power—to get ahead in life. Success is important to me. Money means having control over the things I value most.*

   ❏ *Love—to buy things for others. Relationships are important to me. Money means having the means to express my love to others and to build relationships.*

2. Team up with two or three other people and answer the following questions:

   • What is one way your money tendency impacts you?

   • What is one step you can take to begin limiting that impact?

SAVING AND DEBT

OBJECTIVES

In this session, you will:

1. Complete the savings category of the Spending Plan worksheet.

2. Reflect on who you are becoming as a debtor.

3. Decide on an action step to take concerning the use of credit cards.

4. Complete the debt portion of the Spending Plan worksheet.

Practical Tips on Saving

Savings is:

- Money you _____.

- Not money we have lost or given up.

- Future spending.

The Benefit of Saving

One huge benefit of saving is that it allows the very powerful force of compounding to work in our favor.

Compound interest is:

Interest earning interest, earning interest.

Compound interest example:

- $100 @ 10% = $10 interest

- $110 @ 10% = $11 interest

- The extra $1 is compound interest.

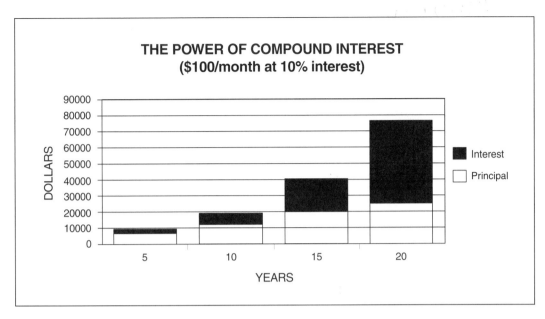

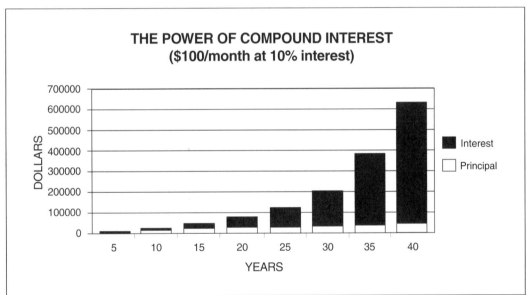

The fruit of the Spirit required here is patience!

There's a cumulative effect of little things over time.

Three Kinds of Savings

_____ savings:

- Prepare you for the unexpected.

- Have three months of basic living expenses (such as housing, food, and transportation costs).

- Should be kept in accounts you have easy access to (like a money market fund).

Replacement savings:

- Are for large, expected purchases.

- Could be invested in short-term certificates of deposit as well as money market funds.

_____ savings:

- Are for planned circumstances that have long time-frames.

- Take advantage of your employer's retirement plan if possible.

Individual Activity: *Spending Plan Application*

1. Calculate an appropriate level of emergency savings. Consider three months of basic living expenses such as housing, food, and transportation.

2. Consider your current financial situation. Set a short-term goal for savings that will help you begin to build your emergency savings fund. If you already have an emergency savings fund, consider goals for replacement or long-term savings.

3. Fill in the savings category on your Spending Plan worksheet.

Prioritizing the Four Uses of Money

 Key Question: If giving is so right and saving is so wise, why are they so hard to do?

Cultural Order:

- Lifestyle

- Debt

- Saving

- Giving

God-honoring Order:

- Giving

- Saving

- Lifestyle

Transitional Order:

- Give . . . something

- Save . . . a little

- Debt . . . maximize repayment

- Lifestyle . . . spartan

Debt

Video: *The Debtor on the Street*

Notes

The Pull of the Culture vs. the Mind and Heart of God

FOOLISH   FAITHFUL

The Pull of
the Culture

The Mind and
Heart of God

Cultural Myth:

"Debt is expected and _____."

The Cautious Debtor is:

One who avoids entering into debt, is careful and strategic when incurring debt, and always repays debt.

Economic danger of debt:

• Compound interest works against you.

Biblical guidelines:

• Repay debt.

Psalm 37:21: *"The wicked borrow and do not repay . . ."*

• _____ debt.

Proverbs 22:7: *"The borrower is servant to the lender."*

Three Spiritual Dangers of Debt:

- Presumes on the future.

> James 4:14: *"You do not even know what will happen tomorrow."*

- Denies God the opportunity to _____.

> Luke 12:30-31 (NLT): *"Those things dominate the thoughts of most people, but your Father already knows your needs. He will give you all you need from day to day if you make the Kingdom of God your primary concern."*

> Ecclesiastes 7:14: *"When times are good, be happy; when times are bad, consider: God has made the one as well as the other."*

- Fosters _____ and greed.

> Luke 12:15 (NLT): *"Beware! Don't be greedy for what you don't have. Real life is not measured by how much we own."*

Practical Tips on Debt

Five kinds of debt:

- Auto

- Home mortgage

- Education

- Business

- _____

"There's no wise use of a credit card."

Credit Card Studies:

- Family spending using a credit card versus cash:

  Amount spent (with a credit card) rose between 20 and 30 percent.

- Pocket camera purchase using cash versus credit card:

  Cash group paid an average of $29.58.

  Credit card group paid an average of $52.67.

Two Reasons Credit Card Users Spend More:

- Using a credit card is psychologically different than using cash.

- No _____ of how much we've charged.

Credit Card Rules:

- Use only for _____ items.

- Pay the balance in full every month.

- If you violate rule one or rule two, cut up your cards.

Credit Card Tips:

- Have only one card.

- Consider the use of a _____ card.

- Consider deducting the amount from your checkbook balance.

Individual Activity: *Credit Cards*

In the space below, write down one action step you want to take with your credit card.

Action Step:

Credit Card Debt and Repayment Example:

You owe $7,200 @ 18.1%		
Minimum Payment = 2% of the balance or $10—whichever is greater		
You Pay	**Total Paid**	**Time (years)**
$ Minimum/month	$23,049	30+
$144/month	$13,397	8
$144+100/month	$ 9,570	3

 Key Question: Is God big enough and are you committed enough to find a little over three dollars a day somewhere in your expenditures that could go to debt repayment?

Principles for Accelerating Debt Repayment:

- Pay off your _____ debt first.

- As a debt is repaid, roll the amount you were paying to the next largest debt.

- Incur no new debt!

You can do it!

Individual Activity: *Spending Plan Application*

1. Using your pre-work information from the "What I Own and What I Owe" sheet, list each of your debts and fill in the monthly minimum payments on your Spending Plan worksheet.

   If you did not complete the pre-work, estimate your monthly minimum payment for each debt.

2. Set a tentative goal for how much additional payment you plan to make each month.

3. Apply this additional payment to your smallest debt.

Debt repayment is a great investment!

- Guaranteed

- Tax free

- Immediate

- High rate of return

Pay off your credit cards!

Video: *Out of Debt*

Notes

SPENDING

OBJECTIVES

In this session, you will:

1. Reflect on "driving your stake" lifestyle-wise.

2. Set short-term goals for the housing, auto/transportation, insurance, household/personal and entertainment spending categories on your Spending Plan worksheets.

3. Identify action steps to reduce expenses in these categories.

58

Spending

The Pull of the Culture vs. the Mind and Heart of God

FOOLISH   FAITHFUL

The Pull of   The Mind and
the Culture   Heart of God

Four Myths:

- "_____ bring happiness."

- "Your possessions define who you are."

- "The more you have, the more you should spend."

- "Spending is a _____."

The Prudent Consumer is:

One who enjoys the fruits of their labor yet guards against materialism.

Three Biblical Financial Principles:

- Beware of idols.

> Romans 1:25: They "worshiped and served created things rather than the Creator."

- Guard against _____.

> Luke 12:15 (NLT): "Beware! Don't be greedy for what you don't have. Real life is not measured by how much we own."

- Be _____.

> Philippians 4:12: "I know what it is to be in need, and I know what it is to have plenty. I have learned the secret of being content in any and every situation, whether well fed or hungry, whether living in plenty or in want."

Contentment with and gratitude for what we have is the antidote to greed and envy.

God wants us to recognize our immeasurable value as his beloved children and to not associate our value with the possession of material things.

When we practice _____ and learn contentment, we become free to be a blessing to others.

Driving Your Stake

 Key Question: Are you willing to "drive your stake" lifestyle-wise?

Driving your stake means:

- There will be a point in time when you declare, "Enough is enough."

- You distinguish between your _____ needs and what the culture says you need.

Individual Activity: *Driving Your Stake Lifestyle-wise*

Use the space below to answer the following question:

"What would it mean for you to drive your stake lifestyle-wise?"

Notes

Housing

Tips for Mortgage/Taxes/Rent:

- Consider the issue of renting versus owning.

- Think _____ of mortgage.

- Beware of basing a mortgage on _____.

- Exercise caution with regard to equity loans.

- Consider an extended household.

Maintenance and Repairs:

- Become a Mr. or a Ms. "Fix-it."

Utilities:

- Control the thermostat.

- Use phones wisely.

- Evaluate options for Internet and cable services.

Individual Activity: *Spending Plan Application*

1. Look at your pre-work sheet for what you currently spend for housing.

    If you didn't complete the pre-work, use your best estimate of housing expenses. The percent guidelines on the Spending Plan worksheet can help you.

2. Consider some of the issues discussed regarding housing. Write down at least one action step that you plan to take under this category.

    Action Step:

3. Set short-term goals for housing expenses, and fill in this category of your Spending Plan worksheet.

Auto/Transportation

Transportation Quiz:

- What is the least expensive car you can own?

  _____

- When is it economically wise to buy a new (never-owned) car?

  _____

- What are the economic advantages to leasing?

  _____

- What is the proper mileage at which it is best to unload the old car?

  _____

Statistics:

Average reliability

Life = 10.2 years

Mileage = 120,000

Average trade-in

Time = 4 years

Mileage = 50,000

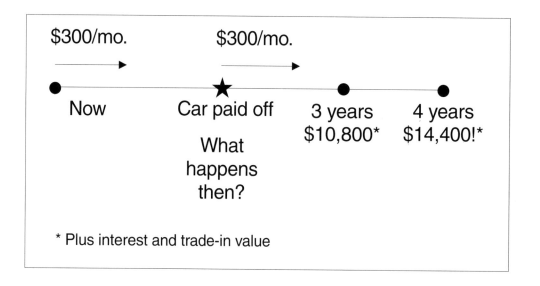

Pay cash for your next car!

Insurance

Auto Insurance Tips:

- Choose the highest deductible you can afford.

  "Catastrophic" is the key word for insurance.

- Shop for it.

- _____ policies.

- Look for other discounts.

- Consider eliminating _____ coverage on an older car.

Life Insurance:

- Consider a renewable term policy.

- Consider whether life insurance is necessary.

Other:

- Consider disability insurance.

- Consider long-term healthcare insurance.

Individual Activity: *Spending Plan Application*

1. Look at your pre-work sheet for what you currently spend on the auto/transportation and insurance categories.

   If you didn't complete the pre-work, use your best estimate of expenses. The percent guidelines on the Spending Plan worksheet can help you.

2. Consider any ways you can to reduce these expenses. Write down at least one action step you plan to take.

   Action Step:

3. Set short-term goals for these categories, and fill in your Spending Plan worksheet.

Household/Personal

Clothing

Books and Magazines

> Philippians 4:8 (NLT): *"Fix your thoughts on what is true and honorable and right. Think about things that are pure and lovely and admirable. Think about things that are excellent and worthy of praise."*

Gambling

Think about what lies behind your gambling, and reflect on what God says in:

- Luke 12:15

- Proverbs 28:19-20

Individual Activity: *Household/Personal and Entertainment Ideas and Spending Plan Application*

1. Look at your pre-work for what you currently spend on the following household/personal expenses: food, clothes/dry cleaning, gifts, books/magazines, allowances, personal technology, and education, and the following entertainment expenses: going out, travel, and other.

    If you didn't complete the pre-work, use your best estimates of expenses. The percent guidelines on the Spending Plan worksheet can help you.

2. Select three categories you think have the most potential to be reduced, and read the information on pages 69–80 pertaining to these expenses. Write down at least one idea that can help you reduce each expense, and set a short-term goal on your Spending Plan worksheet.

    ### Ideas:

3. Set goals for all remaining household/personal and entertainment expenses.

Food

Groceries can be a budget maker. There are a number of tips for reducing your grocery bill:

- Plan menus.
- Make a list.
- Use coupons.
- Buy generic.
- Buy bulk.
- Shop at discounted food stores.
- Beware of marketing techniques.
- Avoid convenience foods.
- Buy in season.
- Plant a garden.
- Eliminate snack foods.

Planning meals for a week or more in advance (particularly in conjunction with advertised sales) and making a list before going to the store and sticking to it are particularly effective ways to control food costs.

Saving money on food does not mean sacrificing nutritional value. In fact, many of the items which are comparatively most expensive (snack foods, sugared cereals, soft drinks, etc.) have the least nutritional value. You can eat inexpensively and healthfully.

Government Statistics on Monthly Food Costs				
Family Size	Thrifty	Low Cost	Moderate	Liberal
2	$248	$329	$405	$475
4	$410	$525	$650	$790

Proof that significant savings can occur in the food budget is reflected in the government statistics above showing the amount spent for food on a monthly basis by families that are thrifty versus those that are liberal in their spending. Almost twice as much is spent on food by the liberal shoppers. This is a key area of the budget at which to look very carefully.

*Source: USDA Center for Nutrition, U.S. average, October 2000.

Clothes/Dry Cleaning

Would you believe the following statistics?

- Ten percent of clothing gets worn 90 percent of the time.
- One-third of clothing never gets worn.

These statistics may be true because we bring new clothes home and they don't look the same under our lighting as they did in the store, they don't match an outfit the way we thought they would, they don't fit quite right, or we just didn't need them in the first place.

It's amazing how few clothes one could really get by on. If you had three pairs of pants, three shirts, and three pieces of outerwear like jackets or sweaters, and if they mixed and matched, you could have twenty-seven different outfits.

Consider shoes. How many pairs of shoes does one really need? We now manufacture shoes to walk slowly in, shoes to walk fast in, shoes to jog in, shoes to run in, etc.

The point here is buy sensibly. Buy styles that last, and look for ways to mix and match color schemes.

Here are some additional tips on clothing:

- Challenge yourself to make it through a season change without buying new clothes unless absolutely necessary.
- Buy during the off-season.
- Shop at discount stores.
- Welcome hand-me-downs.
- Buy non-name brand clothing.*
- Trade outgrown children's clothes with other families.
- Buy fabrics that don't require expensive dry cleaning.

*Interesting note: In a February 2000 *National Geographic* article, the author reported on his visit to a clothing plant in the Chinese city of Birobdzhau in which a "woman was sewing labels into identical blouses. Both labels listed the recommended U.S. retail price. One said, "Old Navy $18"; the other, "Chaps Ralph Lauren $38." The manufacturing costs for each were identical: $5 for labor and $2.50 for material . . ."

Gifts

Many people are surprised at how much they spend on gifts when they list everybody they buy a gift for and how much they tend to spend for anniversaries, birthdays, and Christmas. It adds up and can be a significant item in the budget. And the ironic thing is that we often are creating financial stress on ourselves to buy gifts for folks who already have everything they need and a lot more besides.

There are lots of ideas for reducing your gift expenditures:

- Make or bake gifts.

- Invite people for a special meal.

- Write a letter of appreciation to the person (what do you really appreciate about them and your relationship to them) rather than buying a gift.

- Give to a charity in a person's name. The money goes where it's really needed, and the person knows they've been thought of.

- Give coupons for doing things for someone like chores, backrubs, etc.

- Shop at low-cost stores.

- Make agreements between families to limit the amount spent, the number of persons to whom gifts are given, etc. Draw names from a hat to determine who you'll give to.

The key principle is that cost of the gift is not a reflection of your love.

> *"Not only are the best things in life free,*
> *the best things in life aren't things."*
> Author unknown

Books/Magazines

We've already spoken to the fact that the cheapest subscription in the world is still not a bargain if we never get around to reading the material. We also cautioned to be sure the content is appropriate and fills our minds with the kinds of things mentioned in Philippians 4:8.

In addition, consider the following cost-saving possibilities:

- Share subscriptions with a friend or neighbor.

- Utilize the services of your library . . . get a return on your taxes.

- Buy paperbacks instead of hardcover books.

- Utilize free web sites to gain access to material that appears in periodicals and newspapers.

Allowances

Age four or five is not too young for children to learn the basic biblical principles for handling their money. But for children to learn to handle money wisely, they must have some with which to work. Allowances can be the means by which they receive money and can be an excellent teaching tool.

Here's a technique a man, John, used to use with his small children. Once a month he sat them down, and they would talk about their allowance. He would give each of them their allowance of one dollar in ten dimes. He would also give them each ten paper cups. On each cup, he would write what the cups represented. He'd take the money and count it out while the kids got all excited. Then, he'd ask them, "Did you do your chores this week? Did you honor Mom and Dad? Then, he told them he was going to give them their allowance. He'd say, "Here's the first dime. Where does it go? Put it right in the cup—gifts for Jesus." Where does the second dime go? Savings. You should always save something of what you receive. Where does the third dime go? Take the dime and put it in the food cup. Your food right now can be bubble gum or candy. Where's the fourth dime go? Housing. You've got to have shelter, and shelter costs money. But as long as you're living with Mom and me, you can take the money for shelter and put it into savings." The next three cups went to gifts for others like Father's Day, Mother's Day, or birthdays for brothers or sisters. The last three cups were for whatever they wanted to do.

These same kids then graduated to more advanced tools like a written budget with categories for things like school lunch and gym shoes. They are now in high school and are using Quicken software to budget their money.

Other families have used similar ideas and given their children three banks, one each for giving, saving, and spending. Each bank received a portion of any money the child obtained.

An excellent resource with many additional ideas is *Raising Debt-Proof Kids* by Mary Hunt.

Personal Technology

With technology changing so rapidly, it is easy to get caught up in the "need" to have the latest and greatest new development. However, if you don't really need it, having the latest technology can be a costly venture. Technology itself doesn't always save time and may in fact take more time than expected. E-mail is a classic example. While it's true that it enables our communication capacity and speed, it's also true that it requires more time to manage. Consider the following hints to hold down costs in this area:

- If you're fairly astute regarding computers, they can be purchased as "refurbished" vs. new. Savings can be hundreds of dollars.

- Utilize free Internet service providers.

- Avoid the most expensive offerings. Models with a slightly slower processor come with a substantial price discount and little or no observable performance penalty.

- When buying computers or Personal Digital Assistants, consider only the hardware offerings that have the broadest software support for the major applications you intend to use.

- Don't spend more than a few hundred dollars trying to upgrade a computer that's more than a few years old; buy a new, stripped-down model instead. It will easily outperform the upgraded old one for many years. (Old computers are not the same as old cars in this regard.)

- Recognize that even if your computer is "old" and no longer state-of-the-art, if it still adequately performs the tasks you bought it for, you don't "need" a new one.

- Separate desire for technology toys from genuine need for the benefits they provide. For example, a Palm Pilot is just a toy unless you really do keep a regular calendar, contact list, and to-do lists.

- Buy the "standards"—most likely to be easiest to use, best supported, etc.

- See if the organization you work for will buy the device for you (often they will).

- Be hesitant to add new "fixed" expenses to your budget. Make sure you really need a monthly cell phone plan, or wireless access, or a cable modem service at home. These will creep up and add up.

- Take the time to research once you determine that you will benefit from a technology purchase. Look for sites to get third-party and owner reviews.

- Use Internet sites that allow for ordering with free overnight shipping and no sales tax.

Education

Precollege

For a variety of reasons, some of us struggle with the decision of private versus public school for our children. This is a very sensitive, even volatile topic. It is mentioned here because of the financial implications of that decision.

In making the decision, recognize that the number one influence on our children's development is what takes place in the home. In light of that, I believe that a foremost goal should be to ensure the environment of the home is protected. Thus a key question is: "Will sending my children to private school put us into a debt situation?"

If the answer is yes and considering the stress that debt causes on a family, it would be difficult under those circumstances to justify paying for private education. This is not an anti-private education statement; it is simply speaking to a financial reality. If you are set on private education, look in your Spending Plan and determine what other sacrifices you are willing to make to fund that education without creating financial stress upon the family.

College

If you want to help your children financially with their college education, start saving early. Allow the cumulative effect of compound interest to work for you. Early on, share with your children that they have a responsibility to assist with their college expenses through money they begin saving in junior high or earlier. Set the goal of having no college debt after graduation. Set the expectation of working ten to fifteen hours per week while in college. No curriculum is so difficult that a student cannot work ten to fifteen hours a week and still have time to study and socialize. That, combined with full-time vacation and summer work, can easily earn $5,000 to $10,000 a year toward expenses.

Understand that there are lots of alternatives to a child going to a four-year, high-price institution right out of high school:

- two-year community college programs

- cooperative programs that alternate periods of study with work experience in which the student can earn a significant portion of the next period's tuition

- working a year before entering college

- serving in the military and attending college afterward using government grants earned by this service

Be very cautious regarding college loans. It has become a common assumption that student loans are a good thing—a low-interest way to finance an education. While interest rates for student loans do tend to be favorable, they are still a form of debt and must be repaid. Too often young couples enter marriage with combined student loans totaling tens of thousands of dollars—a huge financial burden with which to begin married life.

Some college advisors and financial aid officers counsel that the cost of college should not figure into the decision of where to attend. Their line of reasoning is that the higher the cost, the more financial aid the student will qualify for. But the fact that often goes unmentioned is that 85 percent of student financial aid available comes in the form of loans.

Some loans may be necessary, but carefully consider alternatives that minimize loans as you plan for college expenses.

Going Out

Cutting back in entertainment expenditures need not mean punishing ourselves, but simply managing ourselves. You can go out and enjoy yourself, but do it in an economical way. A night out is much more enjoyable if you are not anxiety ridden over how you will pay for it.

Consider the following tips:

- Go out to your favorite expensive restaurant, but go for dessert only. Enjoy the ambiance at a fraction of the cost.

- When eating out, order water with a slice of lemon rather than drinks that cost. The difference in your final bill can be substantial.

- Go to matinee movies, second-run movies, or wait for the video.

- Pack lunches and snacks when going on family outings.

- Trade baby-sitting duties with another family.

- Take advantage of free or low-cost local attractions—free days at museums, park district offerings, library programs, etc.

- Entertain friends in your home. Enjoy a potluck meal together. Play board games. Rediscover how both your relationships and your bank accounts can grow from doing so.

- Walks in the park and drives in the country can provide times of good conversation, relaxation, and in the case of walking, some good exercise.

Travel

With the cost of transportation, lodging, and meals, travel expenses and vacations must be carefully planned for and budgeted . . . or their costs lowered by seeking less expensive alternatives. A key question is: Is two weeks of expensive fun worth fifty weeks (or more!) of anguish over how to pay for it?

Some tips for lowering vacation costs include:

- Take shorter trips.

- Travel in the off season.

- Visit friends or relatives to save on hotel costs.

- Cut food costs by taking food along, traveling with a cooler in the car, staying where breakfast is included in the cost (or at least, where children under twelve eat free).

- Take advantage of savings on the Internet.

- Try camping. It is the experience most often cited as the most cherished childhood memory. See if you can borrow and share equipment with friends. There is no need for all of us to own a tent and other equipment we use only a few times a year.

- Understand that it is not the birthright of every child to go to Disney World . . . nor is it an essential experience for normal growth and development.

Entertainment/Other

The Other area under Entertainment contains several expenses.

A major expense (under Fitness/Sports) can be membership at a fitness center. Care of our bodies is part of biblical stewardship. The question is, "If you are a member of a club, do you use your membership?" If everyone who belonged to a health club actually used it, the lines to get in would be forty deep. Is there a less expensive way to stay in shape?

Hobbies are quite legitimate and good for our psychological well-being. But because we tend to really enjoy our hobbies, the money spent on them can easily get out of hand. Build hobby expenses into the Spending Plan and then stick with it. If your hobby is too expensive, find a less expensive alternative.

BALANCING THE SPENDING PLAN

OBJECTIVES

In this session, you will:

1. Complete the professional services and miscellaneous small cash expenditures categories on your Spending Plan worksheet.

2. Balance your Spending Plan worksheet.

Spending

Professional Services

Child Care:

> Evaluate the financial and relational costs of two working parents.

Other:

> Be an educated consumer.

> Proverbs 1:5: *"Let the wise listen and add to their learning, and let the discerning get guidance."*

- Use good judgment.

- Seek referrals.

- Evaluate progress.

Miscellaneous Small Cash Expenditures

Those small things you pay cash for from day to day.

Individual Activity: *Spending Plan Application*

1. Look at your pre-work sheet for what you currently spend for professional services and miscellaneous small cash expenditures.

   If you didn't complete the pre-work, use your best estimate of these expenses. The percentage guidelines on the Spending Plan worksheet can help you.

2. Consider some of the ideas discussed for these categories. Write down at least one action step you plan to take.

Action Step:

3. Set short-term goals for professional services and miscellaneous small cash expenditures, and fill in these categories on your Spending Plan worksheet.

4. Review your entire Spending Plan worksheet. If there are any categories that you did not have time to complete, do so now.

5. Add up all the expenses on your Spending Plan worksheet. **Complete the box in the lower right-hand corner of the worksheet.**

Adjusting the Spending Plan

Three Possible Outcomes:

- Scenario 1: Income equals expenses

- Scenario 2: Income exceeds expenses

- Scenario 3: Expenses exceed income

Three ways to adjust your Spending Plan if your expenses exceed your income:

1. _____ income.

   Simply increasing income does not deal with the root issue.

2. Sell assets to pay off some debt.

3. _____ expenses.

   - Do I have optional expenses I can eliminate?

   - Do I have variable expenses I can further control and reduce?

   - Can I eliminate any assumptions about my "_____" expenses?

 Key Question: How serious are you?

Individual Activity: *Adjusting the Spending Plan*

A. If income equals or exceeds expenses, prayerfully and carefully review all categories to see if the margin can be increased further, and then reflect on how that margin can best be used to further your goals.

Write down at least one action step you plan to take, and make any adjustments to your Spending Plan worksheet.

Action Step:

B. If your expenses exceed your income, prayerfully and carefully review all the categories to reduce expenses.

Write down at least one action step you plan to take to adjust your Spending Plan. Then, adjust the plan and bring it into balance as best you can.

Action Step:

RECORD KEEPING AND COMMITMENT

OBJECTIVES

In this session, you will:

1. Choose and set up a record-keeping system.

2. Consider the obstacles you may encounter implementing your Spending Plan and chosen record-keeping system.

3. Commit to implementing and keeping records for your Spending Plan.

Record Keeping

A record-keeping system is:

A way to keep track of how much you spend.

Benefits of record keeping:

- Gives accurate data.

- Improves _____.

- Allows for mid-course corrections.

- Provides _____.

The truth about record keeping:

- It's simpler than it seems.

- It takes less time than you think.

- It does not require a Ph.D. in math.

Three Systems:

- Envelope

- Written record

- Electronic

Envelope System

The envelope system is:

A way to tangibly designate money for various expenses.

ENVELOPE SYSTEM

All Income

Master Checking Account

Cash

Envelopes

Notes

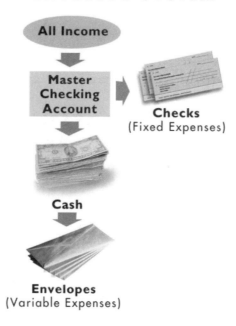

ENVELOPE SYSTEM

All Income

Master Checking Account → **Checks** (Fixed Expenses)

Cash

Envelopes (Variable Expenses)

Notes

Written Record System

Spending Record—Daily Variable Expenses, see next page.

Spending Record Example

Month __January__

Daily Variable Expenses

	Transportation		Household						Professional Services	Entertainment		
	Gas, etc.	Maint/ Repair	Groceries	Clothes	Gifts	Household Items	Personal	Other		Going Out	Travel	Other
(1) Spending Plan	80	40	320	60	80	75	50	—	—	100	70	40
	14	21	9	89	17	14	16	25		22	70	22 (sitter)
	17		87	6	55	22	18			46		
	9		43			9				19		
	19		106			31						
	11		21									
			7									
			13									
(2) Total	70	21	286	95	72	76	34	25	—	87	70	22
(3) (Over)/Under	10	19	34	(35)	8	(1)	16	(25)	—	13	—	18
(4) Last Month YTD												
(5) Total Year to Date												

~~1~~ ~~2~~ ~~3~~ ~~4~~ ~~5~~ ~~6~~ ~~7~~ ~~8~~ ~~9~~ ~~10~~ ~~11~~ ~~12~~ ~~13~~ ~~14~~ ~~15~~ ~~16~~ ~~17~~ ~~18~~ ~~19~~ ~~20~~ ~~21~~ ~~22~~ ~~23~~ ~~24~~ ~~25~~ ~~26~~ ~~27~~ ~~28~~ ~~29~~ ~~30~~ ~~31~~

- Use this page to record expenses that tend to be daily, variable expenses—often the hardest to control.
- Keep receipts throughout the day and record them at the end of the day.
- Total each category at the end of the month (line 2) and compare to the Spending Plan (line 1). Subtracting line 2 from line 1 gives you an (over) or under the budget figure for that month (line 3).
- To verify that you have made each day's entry, cross out the number at the bottom of the page that corresponds to that day's date.
- Optional: If you wish to monitor your progress as you go through the year, you can keep cumulative totals in lines 4 and 5.

Month _January_

Spending Record

Monthly Regular Expenses (generally paid by check once a month)

	Giving		Savings	Debt			Housing				Auto	Insurance		Misc. Cash Exp.
	Church	Other		Credit Cards	Educ.	Other	Mort./Rent	Maint.	Util.	Other	Pmts.	Auto/Home	Life/Med.	
(1) Spending Plan	220	30	155	75	50	—	970	30	180	25	270	90	40	65
	110	20	155	75	50	—	970	0	95 (elec)	44	270	90	40	65
	110	10	200						31 (gas)					
									79 (tel)					
(2) Total	220	30	355	75	50	—	970	0	205	44	270	—	40	65
(3) (Over)/Under	—	—	(200)	—	—	—	—	30	(25)	(19)	—	90	—	—
(4) Last Mo. YTD														
(5) This Mo. YTD														

- This page allows you to record major monthly expenses for which you typically write just one or two checks per month.
- Entries can be recorded as the checks are written (preferably) or by referring back to the check ledger at a convenient time.
- Total each category at the end of the month (line 2) and compare to the Spending Plan (line 1). Subtracting line 2 from line 1 gives you an (over) or under the budget figure for that month (line 3).
- Use the "Monthly Assessment" section to reflect on the future actions that will be helpful in staying on course.

Monthly Assessment

Area	(Over)/Under	Reason	Future Action
Clothes	(35)	After-Christmas sales	No new clothes next month
Savings	(200)	Gift from Aunt Mary	N/A
Utilities	(25)	Electricity and phone	Turn down thermostat
Insurance	90	Quarterly bill next month	N/A

Areas of Victory   Feels great to be ahead on savings. Thanks, Aunt Mary! I'm really proud of how we're doing!

Areas to Watch   Need to look hard at ways to save on electricity and phone bills.

Hints to Make Record Keeping Easier:

- Keep your Spending Record form where you will see it daily.

- _____ to the nearest dollar.

- Combine categories.

- Use "_____ billing."

- Have a miscellaneous cash envelope.

Individual Activity: *Spending Record*

Assume it's the end of the day and you've made some purchases. Using the receipts shown on the next page, fill out the Spending Record form on page 95.

Sample Receipts

Neighborhood Foods
Libertyville

TUE	5/15/00	10:25AM
B. Don Water Gal		1.09
BE Chop Spinach		.83
BE Chop Spinach		.83
Flav Broc-Cau		1.49
Salad Bar		1.50
Carr's Lemon Cremes		2.45
Classico De Napoli		2.79
Sarg Ricotta		2.29
Bays SD Muffins		2.08
Barrilla Lasagna		1.49
Tax 1		.38
Total		17.22

MASON'S PAINTS   126870

DATE 5/15/00

NAME	Carol Larson		
QTY	**DESCRIPTION**	**PRICE**	**AMT**
1	Gal. B. Moore Flat Color #124	$17.99	$17.99
1	Gal. B. Moore Flat Color #643	$17.99	$17.99
	Subtotal		$35.98
		Tax	1.98
	Total		$37.96

.70 soft drink from a machine

MAIN STREET GAS

DLR# 9485588
GURNEE IL

5/15/00
AUTH# 72109
PUMP #2
SPECIAL   9.579G
PRICE/GAL $1.879

FUEL TOTAL $18.00

ABC Department Store

DEPT 196 CL 8	
KNIT JACKET	98.00
PLU DISC 30%	29.40–
NET ITEM PRICE	68.60
DEPT 209 LS 2	
KING LINEN	58.00
PLU DISC 30%	17.40–
NET ITEM PRICE	40.60
SUBTOTAL	109.20
TX IL 8.25%	9.55
TOTAL	118.75
501502000	11:27 AM

Spending Record

Month _____

	Daily Variable Expenses											
	Transportation		Household						Professional Services	Entertainment		
	Gas, etc.	Maint/ Repair	Groceries	Clothes	Gifts	Household Items	Personal	Other		Going Out	Travel	Other
(1) Spending Plan												
1												
2												
3												
4												
5												
6												
7												
8												
9												
10												
11												
12												
13												
14												
15												
16												
17												
18												
19												
20												
21												
22												
23												
24												
25												
26												
27												
28												
29												
30												
31												
(2) Total												
(3) (Over)/Under												
(4) Last Month YTD												
(5) Total Year–to–Date												

- Use this page to record expenses that tend to be daily, variable expenses—often the hardest to control.
- Keep receipts throughout the day and record them at the end of the day.
- Total each category at the end of the month (line 2) and compare to the Spending Plan (line 1). Subtracting line 2 from line 1 gives you an (over) or under the budget figure for that month (line 3).
- To verify that you have made each day's entry, cross out the number at the bottom of the page that corresponds to that day's date.
- Optional: If you wish to monitor your progress as you go through the year, you can keep cumulative totals in lines 4 and 5.

Key Question: Is it worth two minutes a day to bring this crucial area of my life under control?

Electronic System

There are some cautions involved with starting here.

Individual Activity: *Setting Up Your Record-Keeping System*

1. Select which record-keeping system you plan to use to implement your Spending Plan: envelope, written record, or electronic.

2. If you plan on using the written or electronic systems, transfer the numbers from your Spending Plan worksheet to the first lines of the Spending Record form on pages 147 and 148.

    If you plan on using the envelope system, fill in each box under the Envelopes section on page 141, showing the category and dollar amounts. Under the Checks section, write in any expenses you plan to pay with a check.

Implementation Issues

- More than one paycheck per month

- Money building up in accounts

Individual Activity: *Obstacles*

Write down the biggest obstacles you expect to encounter as you implement your Spending Plan and record-keeping system.

Notes

Review and Commitment

FOOLISH   FAITHFUL

The Pull of
the Culture

The Mind and
Heart of God

We become a . . .

- Diligent Earner

- Generous Giver

- Wise Saver

- Cautious Debtor

- Prudent Consumer

Video: *Financial Freedom*

> Notes

Individual Activity: *Becoming Financially Faithful, Financially Free*

Write your answer to the following question:

"If you could become financially faithful and experience real financial freedom, what would your life be like?"

Commitment Plan

- I will begin implementing my Spending Plan and keeping records by _____.

- My accountability partner will be _____.

- I will pray daily for God's guidance and help.

Keeping Your Commitment:

- Commit to using your Spending Plan and record-keeping system for ninety days.

- Do not become discouraged.

- Seek assistance, if needed.

- Pray daily for God's guidance and wisdom.

Summary: God Is Able

He is able, more than able to

> *Accomplish what concerns me today*
>
> *Handle anything that comes my way*
>
> *Do much more than I could ever dream*
>
> *To make me what he wants me to be.*

You can do it!

We want to hear from you. Please send us your comments about the *Good $ense Budget Course* by e-mailing us at gsbudgetcourse@willowcreek.org. Thank you.

APPENDIX

APPENDIX CONTENTS

Forms

EARNING

DETERMINING AN AVERAGE MONTH FOR VARIABLE INCOME

The key to determining a budget in the case of a variable income (due to sales commissions or being self-employed, etc.), is to make a conservative estimate of net income for the coming year. Where possible, this would be done on the basis of the past several years' income. Conservative means not allowing one really good year to unduly influence the estimate for the coming year.

For example, if the past three years' net income were $37,000, $40,000, and 54,000—a really good year!—a conservative estimate for the coming year would be in the range of $44,000, not $56,000. The assumption is that this year may not be the exceptionally good year last year was.

In this example, a monthly budget would be $44,000 divided by 12 or $3,667. In the months when income exceeds $3,667, the excess would be put in a short-term savings account to be drawn on in months when income is less than $3,667.

A wise approach to variable income also includes predetermining the best use of any additional funds, in the event God blesses and actual income exceeds estimated income for the year. Thoughtful consideration before the fact will prevent impulsive decisions if and when the money becomes available, avoiding regrets afterward that it had not been spent in some other, better way.

WHAT HAPPENS TO YOUR RAISES?

Most of the time, the extra money we earn in raises gets used up. A few months later, we're not quite sure where it went. Yet, even a modest raise on a modest salary can add up to a significant amount of additional income in just a few years.

A 4 percent Annual Raise on a $30,000 Salary

	Year 1	Year 2	Year 3
4% raise	$31,200	$32,448	$33,745
Base salary	$30,000	$30,000	$30,000
Additional $ income	$ 1,200	$ 2,448	$ 3,745
Total additional income in three years = $7,393			

Consider the example in the chart above: a $30,000 salary and a 4 percent raise over a three-year period.

• The first year there is a $1,200 increase (4 percent of $30,000).

• The second-year salary is then $32,448, an additional margin of $2,448 from the original salary of $30,000.

• The third-year salary increases to $33,745, producing an increase from the original $30,000 of $3,745.

The total additional income in that three-year period adds up to almost $7,400—nearly one-fourth of the original salary! And that's just a three-year period! Taxes obviously impact the amount not given to charitable causes, but even the after-tax amount accumulates to a significant figure.

Deciding ahead of time how to use raises can be a key part of the strategy for reaching your financial goals.

SAVING

THE CUMULATIVE EFFECT OF LITTLE THINGS OVER AN EXTENDED PERIOD

A faucet dripping once a second can release fifty gallons in one week. In the same way, a slow trickle of money can gradually fill financial reservoirs to overflowing or drain them dry. Since everything we have ultimately belongs to God, every financial splash we make can have eternal significance and consequence. To have the financial freedom God intends, we need to learn how to use—rather than be victimized by—the cumulative effect of little things over an extended period.

To get a clearer picture of this important principle—what the Bible has to say about it and how small financial decisions really do add up—consider the Scriptures and examples below.

What the Bible Says

Scripture is clear in its support of the cumulative effect of a little effort over an extended period.

- "Go to the ant, you sluggard; consider its ways and be wise! . . . it stores its provisions in summer and gathers its food at harvest" (Proverbs 6:6–8).

- "If you have not been trustworthy in handling worldly wealth, who will trust you with true riches?" (Luke 16:11).

- "Everyone who competes in the games goes into strict training. They do it to get a crown that will not last; but we do it to get a crown that will last forever" (1 Corinthians 9:25).

Just a Dollar a Day

The cumulative effect of a little money, just one dollar a day, can be tremendous over a forty-five-year career depending on whether it is saved or added to debt. The chart below compares saving the dollar in a piggy bank, or a tax-sheltered mutual fund with a 10 percent return, versus charging the dollar to a credit card and incurring a 20 percent interest charge.

Years	Piggy bank	Invested in a mutual fund with a 10 percent rate of return	Charged to a credit card with a 20 percent interest rate
5	$1,825	$2,329	−$2,957
10	$3,650	$6,080	−$10,316
15	$5,475	$12,121	−$28,626
20	$7,300	$21,849	−$74,190
25	$9,125	$37,518	−$187,566
30	$10,950	$62,752	−$469,681
35	$12,775	$103,391	−$1,171,674
40	$14,600	$168,842	−$2,918,457
45	$16,425	$274,250	−$7,265,012

Major Purchases

The cumulative effect has a great impact on every major purchase. A $20,000 item can cost as little as $17,700 or as much as $25,500 depending on whether we allow the cumulative effect to work for us by saving for it in advance, or against us by incurring debt to purchase now. Consider this example:

To accumulate $20,000 in five years at 5 percent interest monthly payments to ourselves will have to be $295 and the total of the sixty payments will be $17,700.	To borrow $20,000 for five years at 10 percent interest monthly payments to the finance company will have to be $425 and the total of the sixty payments will be $25,500.

Start Young

Although students and young adults may not feel they have much in the way of assets, the greatest asset they have is *time.*

Saving $100 a month during the first fifteen years of a career, and then saving nothing more for the next twenty-five years with a 10 percent return, results in savings of $431,702.

Saving nothing during the first fifteen years of a career, and then saving $100 a month for the next twenty-five years with a 10 percent return, results in savings of $123,332.

It's Never Too Late

It's never too late to start making a little extra effort. For example, a $100,000 home loan for thirty years at 7 percent interest would have a monthly payment of $665, and the final cost of the loan would be double what was borrowed. However, paying just a little extra every month could dramatically reduce the total cost of the loan.

Extra Payment	Out of Debt	Total Interest
$0/month	30 years	$139,511
$25/month	<27 years	$121,296
$50/month	<24 years	$107,856
$100/month	<21 years	$ 89,003

DEBT

ESTABLISHING A DEBT REPAYMENT PLAN

1. **Establish a Spending Plan based on a temporary, spartan lifestyle.**
   This frees up every possible dollar for the top priority of debt reduction.

2. **Determine whether any nonessential assets can be sold.**
   Cash from the sale of assets can be used to give the debt repayment process a kick-start and provide the initial buffer to ensure success.

3. **List your debts from smallest to largest.**
   Do not pay attention to the interest rate of the debt.

4. **Pay the minimum payment on all debts and the maximum additional possible on the smallest.**
   The goal is to pay off smaller debts quickly. This will give a sense of accomplishment as well as simplify the process as the number of creditors is reduced. Although one could argue that the greatest overall savings would occur by paying off the highest interest debt first, the psychological impact of getting some debts paid quickly far exceeds the downside of the few additional interest dollars it may cost. When only debts of relatively the same amount remain to be paid, apply extra payment to the one with the highest interest.

5. **As each debt is paid off, roll the total amount you were paying to the next largest debt.**
   Add that amount to the minimum payment you were making.

6. **Continue this strategy until all debts are paid.**
   Do not reduce the total amount going to debt repayment as some debts are paid off. It is the "snowball" effect of rolling the previous payment into the next largest debt that gives this system its power.

7. **Incur no new debt, period!**

Discipline will be necessary in this regard. Obviously, you will not make progress if you are continuing to incur new debt as you are attempting to pay off the old. Be creative. Have someone hold you accountable. Ask for God's help. Know in your heart you are doing the right thing.

8. **Discard credit cards.**
   Get rid of them. If you must have a card for travel or emergency, have only one.

9. **Reward yourself occasionally but modestly.**
   As progress is made and milestones are reached, it is appropriate to reward yourself. For some, the progress itself may be reward enough.

The following page shows a sample Debt Reduction Plan and an explanation for each column. A blank Debt Reduction Plan is included in the Forms section on page 137.

Sample Debt Reduction Plan

Item	Amount Owed	Interest	Minimum Monthly Payment	Additional Payment $ 150	Payment Plan and Pay-off Dates				
					3 Months	6 Months	15 Months	22 Months	26 Months
Sears	$372	18.0	$15	$165	paid!				
Doctor	$550	0	$20	$20	$185	paid!			
Visa	$1980	19.0	$40	$40	$40	$225	paid!		
Master	$2369	16.9	$50	$50	$50	$50	$275	paid!	
Auto	$7200	6.9	$259	$259	$259	$259	$259	$534	paid!
Total	$12,471		$384	$534	$534	$534	$534	$534	0

- The first and second columns list to whom the debt is owed and the amount owed. Debts are listed in the order of lowest to highest amount.
- The third and fourth columns list the interest rate and the minimum monthly payment for each debt.
- The fifth column indicates the amount of additional payment above the minimum that can be made and adds that amount to the minimum payment for the first (smallest) debt listed.
- The remaining columns show how, as each debt is paid, the payment for it is rolled down to the next debt. Pay-off dates can be calculated in advance or simply recorded as they are achieved.

SPENDING

WHEN IS ENOUGH, ENOUGH?

The Bible doesn't give absolute guidelines for deciding when enough is enough, but the following nine principles can provide guidance for making wise financial decisions or evaluating a desire to purchase something.

1. Start with the right attitude: everything you have was created by God, is owned by God, and is to be used for God's purposes.

2. If the desire seems reasonable to mature Christian brothers and sisters whose discernment you respect, it is usually wise.

3. If the desire arises from pain over the plight of the poor, the unfortunate, or the disenfranchised, it is likely to be Spirit led and honoring to God.

4. If the desire involves the well-being of children, it is often right.

5. If the desire is primarily one of wanting to improve your own living conditions or lifestyle, you should not automatically assume it is wrong.

6. Consider whether the desire springs from an incompleteness in your relationship with Christ. Are you trying to fill with purchases an empty place in your heart?

7. Consider whether the resources of God's creation would be adequate to provide for all of his children the thing you desire for yourself.

8. Evaluate how important your desire seems in the context of your own mortality. Ask, "How important will this purchase seem to me when I am on my deathbed?"

9. Ask, "What would Jesus do in my situation?"

Points two through six adapted from *Freedom of Simplicity,* Richard J. Foster (HarperCollins, San Francisco, 1981), pages 88-89.

NOTHING DOWN, NOTHING A MONTH

Dave Ramsey

One way products and services are sold is by offering consumers unbelievable financing. Have you ever heard of "ninety days same as cash" or "no finance charges until January" or "no-interest financing"? Did it ever occur to you that in a world driven by money markets, a company offering zero interest with no ulterior motive would soon go broke?

Here is how it really works. First, the product is priced higher to cover the expense of the zero-interest financing. So there is actually no savings to begin with. But the story just starts there. Most dealers then sell the financing contract to a finance company to buy. And why would a finance company buy a contract at zero interest? Because the dealer (a furniture store, department store, electronics store, etc.)—who marked the item up in the first place—sells the financing contract to the finance company at a discount. Everyone but the purchaser wins. The dealer got what they wanted—an immediate sale at a regular profit (after the discount to the finance company). And when the buyer pays off the finance company, the finance company makes a profit because they got the buyer's contract at a discount from the dealer.

Second, and more importantly, over 70 percent of the time *the buyer does not pay off the dealer within the stated period.* Then the finance company gladly begins to charge interest and initiates a longer payment plan. When this occurs, the buyer often pays over 24 percent interest (if that state allows it) and the contract is on prepaid interest or "rule of 78's," which means there is a huge prepayment penalty. Plus, the company will add interest for the original ninety days, which is only "free" if paid off within the ninety days. They also typically will sell overpriced life and disability insurance to pay off their overpriced loan should something happen to your overpriced self. I once met a man who had life insurance on a loan against a rototiller!

This brilliant zero-interest plan now has turned into one of the worst financial decisions ever made because of the total cost of that item. A $1,000 couch at 25 percent for three years with credit life and disability insurance can end up costing at least $1,900.

Adapted from *Financial Peace,* Dave Ramsey (Viking Press, New York, 1992, 1997), pages 39-40.

A BIG DIFFERENCE IN A SHORT TIME

Question: I'm determined to be a better steward of God's resources. It would be an encouragement to me if I could do something that would make a big difference in a short time. Do you have a suggestion?

Answer: Except for housing (an expense that is pretty hard to change), cars are the biggest drain on most budgets. The average price of a new car in the United States is $19,000. Although cars remain reliable for an average of ten years and 120,000 miles, Americans tend to keep cars an average of only four-and-half years and 41,000 miles. Hanging on to your present car—or buying a good used car instead of a new one—may be the "one big thing" you could do to free up a significant amount of money for higher purposes.

Here are some facts you might consider when you decide whether having an older car is appropriate for you:

- A car loses most of its trade-in value in the first four years. If you trade in a new car after four years or less, you're paying a tremendous price for less than half the useful life of the car. On the other hand, if you buy a good used vehicle, you can get more than half the useful life of the car at a relatively thrifty price.

- We typically assume that new cars are more reliable than used cars. However, according to *Consumer Reports,* cars less than one year old make as many trips to the repair shop as cars that are four or five years old. The most reliable years of a car's life are the second and third years.

- When you select a new car, you have to base your decision on the manufacturer's claims, but used cars have a track record you can check. Most libraries have the *Consumer Reports Annual Buying Guide,* which has a chapter called "Ratings of Cars as Used Cars," and a huge chart giving "Six-Year Repair Records" for most models. Also, the National Highway Traffic Safety Administration has a toll-free hotline you can use to check to see if a used car has ever been recalled: (800) 424-9393.

- As a car gets older, the costs for gas and oil increase, but the costs for collision and theft insurance decrease.

- New car dealers typically save the best trade-in cars to sell on their own used car lots. These cars are often thoroughly checked and backed by a used car warranty. In some cases, used car buyers may even inherit the remainder of the manufacturer's new car warranty.

- Recently, leasing has become a popular option and is pushed heavily by many auto dealers. No wonder—it's a good deal for them. The appeal to many unsuspecting folks is the lower monthly payment. Payments should be lower—at the end of the lease you don't own anything! The up side for used car buyers is that an increasing number of leased cars are being turned in at the end of the lease and then turn up on used car lots.

Bottom Line:

- A recent comparison of the cost differential of keeping a four-year-old car for another four years and spending more on gas, oil, tires, and maintenance versus buying a new car showed the savings in keeping the four-year-old car to be over $5,000…assuming the new car would be paid for in cash. Add a couple thousand more dollars if it would be financed.

- A comparison of buying a two-year-old used car and keeping it for eight years versus leasing a new car every three years over a "driving lifetime" of forty-eight years revealed a staggering (almost unbelievable) differential of over $400,000.

You might quibble over some of the assumed costs, and the equation might change by some thousands of dollars, but the point is clear—huge savings are possible in the area of automobiles.

When Jesus spoke about avoiding "treasures on earth, where moth and rust destroy and where thieves break in and steal," he could have been speaking of cars. Probably his advice to Christian families today would be, "Keep the heap," and "Store up for yourselves treasures in heaven, where moth and rust do not destroy and where thieves do not break in and steal. For where your treasure is, there your heart will be also" (Matthew 6:19-21).

Information on costs and savings taken from "A Big Difference in a Short Time," by Jon Kopke, *College Hill Presbyterian Church Belltower News* (November, 1996).

UNPLUGGING FROM THE CONSUMPTIVE SOCIETY

"There are two ways of getting enough; one is to continue to accumulate more of it, the other is to desire less." *

Here are ten tips on simplifying life and being a good steward.

1. **Know where your money goes—develop a budget.**
   If we make no more than $25,000 per year for forty-five working years, we will have been the stewards of $1,125,000! How dare we consider handling that amount of money without keeping records and knowing where it went! Also, treat the giving portion of your budget differently than your operating budget. The goal of the operating budget is to hold down expenditures, but the goal of giving is to increase expenditures.

2. **Actively reject the advertising industry's persuasive and pervasive attempt to squeeze you into its mold.**
   Greet with sarcastic laughter all the patently false claims of phony TV commercials. Have your family shout in unison, "Who do you think you're kidding?" The goal of advertising is to create a desire for products. This is often done by creating dissatisfaction with what you now have, even though it may be quite satisfactory. Avoid settings that subject you to these overt efforts to create a mindset that is antithetical to Christ's teachings. Don't watch ads on TV. Don't read mail-order catalogs. Don't window shop in malls. Look at advertisements only after you have carefully determined your need for a particular product, and then only to seek the best quality at the lowest price.

3. **When you do decide it is right to purchase an item, see if God will provide it without you having to buy it.**
   Pray about it for a week, then consider if you still need it. If God hasn't provided it and you do still need the item, go ahead and purchase it. This practice integrates our needs with the concept of God's provision and has the additional benefit of avoiding impulse buying.

* Source of quote unknown.

4. **Stress the quality of life above quantity of life.**
Refuse to be seduced into defining life in terms of having, rather than being. Learn the wonderful lesson that to increase the quality of life means to decrease material desire—not vice versa.

5. **Make recreation healthy, happy, and gadget free.**
Consider noncompetitive games—why must there always be a winner? Avoid "spectatoritis." Modern spectator sports programs are obscene in their waste of human and material resources. It is a joy to watch some games, but addiction to doing so is another thing altogether. Develop the habit of homemade celebrations. Read together, play games, tell stories, have skits, invite other families in (and don't kill yourself preparing for them).

6. **Learn to eat sensibly and sensitively.**
Eliminate prepackaged dinners. Plan menus ahead, and buy only to meet the menu. Eliminate nonnutritious snack foods. Be conscious of the bio food chain. Grain-fed animals that require ten pounds of grain to produce one pound of meat are a luxury that the bio food chain cannot sustain for the masses of humanity. Get in on the joy of gardening. Dwarf fruit trees can supply large quantities of fresh fruit. Explore food cooperatives. Eat out less and make it a celebration when you do. Go without food one day a month and give the money you save to the poor. Buy less food rather than diet pills!

7. **Learn the difference between significant travel versus self-indulgent travel.**
Give your travel purpose. Travel inexpensively. Become acquainted with people as well as places.

8. **Buy things for their usefulness, not their status.**
Clothes can be quite presentable but inexpensive. Furniture can be used, refinished. Significant amounts of money can be saved buying good used cars and less expensive models. Are you alone after having raised your family? Consider inviting extended family, a college student, or single young person to live with you.

9. **Learn to enjoy things without owning them.**
Possession is an obsession in our culture. If we own it, we feel we can control it, and if we control it, we feel it will give us more pleasure. This is an illusion. Enjoy the beauty of the beach without the

compulsion to buy a piece of it. Many things can be shared among neighbors and friends. Give some things away just for the freedom it brings.

10. **Teach your children by word and deed about the varied uses of money. Provide clear guidelines about what you consider reasonable and unreasonable expenditures.**

Culture trains children to desire everything in sight when they enter a store. You do them no favor when you give in to their incessant demands. Get them what they need, not what they want; and in time, they will come to want what they need. Provide children with the experience of a growing self-governance. At a young age, offer them an allowance to give them the experience of saving and giving away, and decide with them how to spend the rest. In time, as their allowances and earning abilities grow, go one-half with them on necessities. Eventually, let them pay for everything themselves. Consider the goal of handling all income and expenses except for food and housing by age sixteen and financial independence, except for college expenses, by age eighteen. Consider approaching the cost of college as the young adult's responsibility, with parents acting as a safety net, as opposed to the cost of college being the parents' responsibility, with the young adult chipping in what they can—a very significant difference in philosophy.

* Adapted from *Celebration of Discipline*, Richard J. Foster, (HarperCollins, San Francisco, 1978, 1988, 1998), pages 78-83.

RECORD KEEPING

KEEPING MONTH-TO-DATE AND YEAR-TO-DATE TOTALS ON THE SPENDING RECORD

Often it can be helpful to know how you are doing in various categories not just for the current month but from the beginning of the Spending Plan year.

Lines 4 and 5 on the Spending Record provide that information.

Line 4 carries forward the amount each category was over or under the Spending Record from the month before. If this is done each month, and that figure is added to the over or under figure for the current month, the resulting figure represents the status of that category up to this point in the current budget year. In some cases, it may be of little interest to track certain accounts because they never vary from budget, and discipline is exercised in that area. But consider three categories of variable expenses—groceries, clothes, and going out—that have been tracked in the example on page 125.

This current month groceries were $34 under Spending Plan. A total of $320 was allocated but only $286 was spent. In previous months, a total of $118 (line 4) less than what had been allocated was actually spent. That amount, added to the $34 under for this month, gives a Year-to-Date (YTD) total of $152 under the budget (line 5). The food category is in good shape for the year.

The clothing category is $35 over budget for this month and $142 over for the year at the end of last month. As a result, this category is now $177 over for the year to date.

The going out category is $13 under the allotment for this month but was $96 over the allotment prior to this month. That means this category is $83 over the budget for the year.

This cumulative data can be very helpful as the year progresses. In this situation, if the holiday season were approaching, money would be available in the grocery category to have guests over for some nice holiday meals and still stay within the food budget for the year.

On the other hand, since the clothing category is over budget, it might be a good idea to pass the hint to others that it would be nice to get clothing gifts for Christmas! Moderation in the "going out" category is also in order to bring that Spending Plan category back into budget.

Spending Record Example

Month __October__

Daily Variable Expenses

	Transportation		Household						Professional Services	Entertainment		
	Gas, etc.	Maint/Repair	Groceries	Clothes	Gifts	Household Items	Personal	Other		Going Out	Travel	Other
(1) Spending Plan	80	40	320	60	80	75	50	—	—	100	70	40
	14	21	9	89	17	14	16	25		22	70	22 (sitter)
	17		87	46	55	22	18			46		
	9		43			9				19		
	19		106			31						
	11		21									
			7									
			13									
(2) Total	70	21	286	95	72	76	34	25	—	87	70	22
(3) (Over)/Under	10	19	34	(35)	8	(1)	16	(25)	—	13	—	18
(4) Last Month YTD			118	(142)						(96)		
(5) Total Year to Date			152	(177)						(83)		

~~1~~ ~~2~~ ~~3~~ ~~4~~ ~~5~~ ~~6~~ ~~7~~ ~~8~~ ~~9~~ ~~10~~ ~~11~~ ~~12~~ ~~13~~ ~~14~~ ~~15~~ ~~16~~ ~~17~~ ~~18~~ ~~19~~ ~~20~~ ~~21~~ ~~22~~ ~~23~~ ~~24~~ ~~25~~ ~~26~~ ~~27~~ ~~28~~ ~~29~~ ~~30~~ ~~31~~

- Use this page to record expenses that tend to be daily, variable expenses—often the hardest to control.
- Keep receipts throughout the day and record them at the end of the day.
- Total each category at the end of the month (line 2) and compare to the Spending Plan (line 1). Subtracting line 2 from line 1 gives you an (over) or under the budget figure for that month (line 3).
- To verify that you have made each day's entry, cross out the number at the bottom of the page that corresponds to that day's date.
- Optional: If you wish to monitor your progress as you go through the year, you can keep cumulative totals in lines 4 and 5.

IMPLEMENTATION ISSUES

More Than One Paycheck per Month

Item	Spending Plan ($)	1st Paycheck ($)	2nd Paycheck ($)
✓ Giving	250	125	125
✓ Saving	155		155
✓ Mortgage	970	970	
✓ Utilities	180		180
✓ Telephone	55		55
✓ Auto Payment	270		270
✓ Debt Repayment	110		110
Clothes	60		60
Gifts	80		80
Gas	80	40	40
Food	320	160	160
Household Misc.	75	30	45
Entertainment	100	50	50
Misc. Small Exp.	45		45
Total	**2,750**	**1,375**	**1,375**

✓ = paid by check

Making a one-time plan for how each paycheck will be allocated and simply referring to it each payday can be a wonderful way to ease the anxiety over questions like, "Which bill do I pay now?" and "Do I have enough for food and gas?"

In the above example, the person receives net take-home pay of $2,750 per month and is paid twice a month ($1,375 per pay period). The first column represents the Spending Plan for this family. They give $250 per month, save $155, have a mortgage payment of $970, etc.

Out of the first paycheck, checks are written for half of the monthly giving and for the mortgage. The rest of the check is used for half of the allocation for gas, food, entertainment, and a portion of household/miscellaneous.

Out of the second paycheck, checks are written for the other half of giving, all short-term savings, utilities, telephone, auto payment, and debt repayment. The remainder of that check covers the other half of gas, food, household items, entertainment, and the total for the monthly miscellaneous cash expenditures category.

In developing such a plan, it may be necessary to adjust some payment dates to balance out payments from the two checks. Once the plan has been devised, a copy can be kept with your checkbook, and it will eliminate any question about how each paycheck is to be used.

MONEY BUILDING UP IN ACCOUNTS

Once you begin placing money for certain categories that tend to build up over time into a short-term savings account, the question arises, "I have this savings account, and it has an amount of money in it, but how do I tell how much is for what category?"

The ledger sheet on page 130 shows an example to help answer this question. It is a ledger for a money market fund that contains short-term savings that have accumulated for several budgeting categories.

At the top, there is a description of the four funds into which money is being deposited each payday. In this case, the money is for emergencies, vacations, gifts, and auto repair. Lines 1 through 6 on the form are explained below.

Line 1 is the balance brought forward ($3,500) from the previous year. Based on the activity of that year, $2,100 of that $3,500 belongs to the Emergency account, $500 belongs to the Vacation account, $300 belongs to the Gift account, and $600 belongs to the Auto Repair account.

Lines 2 through 6 show the activity in the fund for the most recent month. On January 8, Dan bought Wendy a birthday gift. He entered $40 in the total balance column with a parenthesis around it indicating that it is an amount they need to subtract from the balance because they just spent $40. The $40 was also shown as being spent from the Gift fund.

On January 15, Dan got paid. He deposited $235 to the fund, so $235 is shown under the Total Balance column. Of that $235, $100 was for the Emergency fund, $70 was for the Vacation fund, $30 was for the Gift fund, and $35 was for the Auto Repair fund. They show those four figures under each of those funds. Since this was money being added to the funds, the figures do not have parentheses around them.

On January 17, Joe's Transmission Shop hit them hard with a $500 transmission job. They paid that out of their Auto Repair fund.

On January 25, they bought Sam and Mary a wedding present and recorded a $50 deduction from the total column, and a $50 deduction from the gift column.

On January 30, another paycheck was again distributed among the four categories.

The last line shows end-of-the-month totals based on adding and subtracting the transactions. The fund now has a total of $3,380 distributed as shown.

On page 139 is a blank form on which you can set up your own ledger to track savings.

Month _January_

Wendy and Dan's Money Market Fund for Short-Term Savings

	Date	Description	Total Fund Balance	Fund #1 Emergency	Fund #2 Vacation	Fund #3 Gift	Fund #4 Auto Repair	Fund #5
1	12/31	Previous year balance forward	3500	2,100	500	300	600	
2	1/8	Wendy's birthday gift	(40)			(40)		
3	1/15	Paycheck	235	100	70	30	35	
4	1/17	Joe's transmission	(500)				(500)	
5	1/25	Sam and Mary's wedding	(50)			(50)		
6	1/30	Paycheck	235	100	70	30	35	
		End of month total	3380	2300	640	270	170	

RECOMMENDED RESOURCES

BOOKS

Randy Alcorn, *Money, Possessions and Eternity*. Tyndale House Publishers, 1989.
Excellent integration of biblical truths and practical ways to live them out. Very challenging.

Ron Blue, *Master Your Money*. Thomas Nelson, 1997.
Nuts and bolts information and forms presented in a biblical context.

Richard Foster, *Freedom of Simplicity*. HarperSanFrancisco, 1998.
First published in 1981, this book is classic. An excellent resource for the person seeking to understand biblical stewardship at a deeper level. Foster points the way to finding harmony in a complex world through understanding simplicity.

Mary Hunt, *Mary Hunt's Debt-Proof Your Kids*. Broadman and Holman Publishers, 1998.
An excellent, hard-hitting book with lots of straight talk and good ideas for debt-proofing kids. Hunt also publishes the *Cheapskate Monthly* newsletter, that can be ordered by calling 800-550-3502.

Linda Kelly, *Two Incomes and Still Broke?* Crown Publishing, 1998.
The author introduces "new math" to show that there are many hidden costs involved with second incomes. She also provides advice and worksheets that enable a family to accurately assess the financial pros and cons of two incomes.

Austin Pryor, *Sound Mind Investing, Revised Edition*. Victor Books, 2000.
Pryor does an excellent job of presenting thoroughly researched material on a complex topic in layperson's terms . . . and does it all from a Christian perspective. However, don't even think about reading this book until consumer debt is repaid and a savings plan is in place! Austin also

publishes a monthly newsletter that can be obtained from his web site: www.soundmindinvesting.com.

David Ramsey, *Financial Peace*. Viking Press, 1992, 1997.
Lots of practical advice on avoiding "stuffitis" and learning how present sacrifice can produce long-term peace.

Juliet Schor, *The Overspent American*. HarperCollins, 1998.
A secular commentary that examines why so many of us feel materially dissatisfied in the midst of plenty. This Harvard economist looks at the plight of the consumer in the midst of a culture in which spending has become the ultimate social act.

Dallas Willard, *The Spirit of the Disciplines*. HarperSanFrancisco, 1991.
Chapter ten, "Is Poverty Spiritual?" is a powerful commentary on how to look at one's financial state from a biblical perspective. As quoted by Willard, "We need to reject both glorified aestheticism and sanctified consumerism."

AUDIO TAPES

The following audio tapes may be obtained by calling (800)570-9812 or by logging on to www.willowcreek.com.

M0042	John Ortberg	*It All Goes Back in the Box*
C9516	John Ortberg	*What Jesus Really Taught about Greed*
C9819	John Ortberg	*A Reward Worth Living For*
M9402	Bill Hybels	*The Truth about Earthly Treasures*
C9122	Bill Hybels	*The Gift of Giving*
M9820	Bill Hybels	*Words to the Rich*
AM9603	Bill Hybels	Achieving Financial Freedom (four-part series)
M9902	Bill Hybels	*Money, Sex, and Power: Who Owns What*

M9903	Bill Hybels	*Money, Sex, and Power: The Financial Ten Commandments*
M9949	Bill Hybels	*Truths that Transform, Part 9: Learn to Be Content in All Circumstances*
DF9906	Bill Hybels/ Dick Towner	*Establishing Financial Good $ense*

WEB SITES

www.bankrate.com
Lists certificate-of-deposit rates paid by banks throughout the country.

www.moneynet.com
Lists the seven-day annualized yields of the largest money market mutual funds open to individuals.

www.kbb.com
Lists Kelly Blue Book car values.

www.ssa.gov/retire
Provides online retirement income calculations. New calculators are being developed almost weekly. Also check the web sites of large brokerage houses.

www.ambest.com
Insurance company ratings by one of the industry's top rating services.

www.debtfree.org
Features a debt calculator to help you figure the amount of time needed to pay off a debt.

www.debtorsanonymous.org
The official site of the Debtors Anonymous Organization.

ADDITIONAL RESOURCES

Consumer Credit Counseling Service
Provides low-cost debt counseling. Call (800)388-2227 for the nearest location. Web site: www.nfcc.org

Consumer Credit Handbook
Explains how to fix errors on credit reports and what to do if you are turned down for credit. Write to Consumer Information Center, Pueblo, CO 81002.

Debtors Anonymous
Nationwide network of twelve-step groups to help folks with debt and spending addictions. Web site: www.debtorsanonymous.org

National Center for Financial Education
Provides free brochures on how to live debt free. Send self-addressed stamped envelope to P.O. Box 34070, San Diego, CA 92163.

Credit Report
To get a copy of your credit report contact Ecquifax at (800)685-1111 or on their web site: www.equifax.com

FORMS

Included on the following pages are perforated forms you can pull out and use. These include the Debt Reduction Plan, Form for Tracking Short-term Savings, Envelope Record-Keeping Worksheet, an expanded version of the Biblical Financial Principles taught in the course, the Spending Plan, and three copies of the Spending Record.

If you decide to use the written record-keeping system, these forms can be used for the next two months. Feel free to make photocopies of a blank Spending Record to use for subsequent months.

The Biblical Financial Principles are perforated so you can keep them handy and easily refer to them for the Bible's wisdom concerning the use of money.

Debt Reduction Plan

Item	Amount Owed	Interest	Minimum Monthly Payment	Additional Payment $____	Payment Plan and Pay-off Dates				
Total									

- The first and second columns list to whom the debt is owed and the amount owed. Debts are listed in the order of lowest to highest amount.
- The third and fourth columns list the interest rate and the minimum monthly payment for each debt.
- The fifth column indicates the amount of additional payment above the minimum that can be made and adds that amount to the minimum payment for the first (smallest) debt listed.
- The remaining columns show how, as each debt is paid, the payment for it is rolled down to the next debt. Pay-off dates can be calculated in advance or simply recorded as they are achieved.

Month _____

Form for Tracking Short-Term Savings

Date	Description	Total Fund Balance	Fund #1	Fund #2	Fund #3	Fund #4	Fund #5

ENVELOPE RECORD-KEEPING WORKSHEET

Envelopes

The boxes below represent envelopes in which you will place cash for variable expenses each month. For each category, write in the category name (clothing, food, etc.) and the budgeted amount.

Category: _____	Category: _____
$_____	$_____

Category: _____	Category: _____
$_____	$_____

Category: _____	Category: _____
$_____	$_____

Category: _____	Category: _____
$_____	$_____

Checks

Use the entries below to list the monthly regular expenses you will pay by check.

Category _____   Category _____

$_____ $_____

Category _____   Category _____

$_____ $_____

Category _____   Category _____

$_____ $_____

Category _____   Category _____

$_____ $_____

BIBLICAL FINANCIAL PRINCIPLES

FOUNDATION OF THE GOOD SENSE MINISTRY
Cultivate a steward's mindset.

GOD CREATED EVERYTHING
In the beginning there was nothing, and God created (Genesis 1:1).

GOD OWNS EVERYTHING
"The silver is mine and the gold is mine,' declares the LORD Almighty" (Haggai 2:8). "Every animal of the forest is mine, and the cattle on a thousand hills" (Psalm 50:10). "The earth is the Lord's, and everything in it. The world and all its people belong to him." Psalm 24:1 NLT).

Flowing out of the fact that God created and owns everything is the logical conclusion that whatever we possess is not really ours, but belongs to God; we are simply entrusted with our possessions. Therefore, we are trustees, not owners. Although a 1 Corinthians 4 (quoted below) does not directly refer to material possessions, its counsel is applicable to this aspect of life as well.

WE ARE TRUSTEES
"A person who is put in charge as a manager must be faithful" (1 Corinthians 4:1–2 NLT).

WE CAN'T SERVE TWO MASTERS
"No one can serve two masters. For you will hate one and love the other, or be devoted to one and despise the other. You cannot serve both God and money" (Matthew 6:24 NLT).

USE RESOURCES WISELY
"His master replied, 'Well done, good and faithful servant! You have been faithful with a few things; I will put you in charge of many things. Come and share your master's happiness!'" (Matthew 25:21–28).

PURSUE BIBLICAL, FINANCIAL KNOWLEDGE
"Buy the truth and do not sell it; get wisdom, discipline and understanding" (Proverbs 23:23). "Plans fail for lack of counsel, but with many advisers they succeed" (Proverbs 15:22).

MEASURABLE GOALS AND REALISTIC PLANS
"Commit to the LORD whatever you do, and your plans will succeed" (Proverbs 16:3).

TRUSTWORTHINESS MATTERS
"Whoever can be trusted with very little can also be trusted with much, and whoever is dishonest with very little will also be dishonest with much. So if you have not been trustworthy in handling worldly wealth, who will trust you with true riches? And if you have not been trustworthy with someone else's property, who will give you property of your own?" (Luke 16:10–12).

EARNING
The Diligent Earner—One who produces with diligence and purpose and is content and grateful for what he or she has.

God established work while Adam and Eve were yet in the Garden of Eden. God invited them to join him in the ongoing act of caring for creation. Work before the fall of Adam and Eve is a blessing, not a curse. All work has dignity. Our work should be characterized by the following principles.

BE DILIGENT; SERVE GOD
"Whatever you do, work at it with all your heart, as working for the Lord" (Colossians 3:23).

PROVIDE FOR OURSELVES AND THOSE DEPENDENT ON US
"Those who won't care for their own relatives, especially those living in the same household, have denied what we believe. Such people are worse than unbelievers" (1 Timothy 5:8 NLT).

BE GRATEFUL; REMEMBER FROM WHOM INCOME REALLY COMES
"Remember the LORD your God, for it is he who gives you the ability to produce wealth" (Deuteronomy 8:18).

ENJOY YOUR WORK; BE CONTENT IN IT
"It is good for people to eat well, drink a good glass of wine, and enjoy their work—whatever they do under the sun—for however long God lets them live. And it is a good thing to receive wealth from God and the good health to enjoy it. To enjoy your work and accept your lot in life—that is indeed a gift from God" (Ecclesiastes 5:18-19 NLT).

BE TRANSFORMED WORKERS
"Slaves, obey your earthly masters with respect and fear, and with sincerity of heart, just as you would obey Christ. Obey them not only to win their favor when their eye is on you, but like slaves of Christ, doing the will of God from your heart" (Ephesians 6:5-6).

EARN POTENTIAL, SHARE EXCESS
"If you are a thief, stop stealing. Begin using your hands for honest work, and then give generously to others in need" (Ephesians 4:28 NLT).

GIVING
The Generous Giver—One who gives with an obedient will, a joyful attitude, and a compassionate heart.

WE ARE MADE TO GIVE
We are made in the image of God (Genesis 1:26-27). God is gracious and generous. We will lead a more satisfied and fulfilled life when we give to others.

GIVE AS A RESPONSE TO GOD'S GOODNESS
"Every good and perfect gift is from above" (James 1:17). Therefore, we give out of gratefulness for what we have received.

GIVE TO FOCUS ON GOD AS OUR SOURCE AND SECURITY
"But seek first his kingdom and his righteousness and all these things will be given to you as well" (Matthew 6:33).

GIVE TO HELP ACHIEVE ECONOMIC JUSTICE
"Our desire . . . is that there might be equality. At the present time your plenty will supply what they need" (2 Corinthians 8:13-14). Throughout Scripture, God expresses his concern for the poor and calls us to share with those less fortunate.

GIVE TO BLESS OTHERS
"I will make you into a great nation and I will bless you; I will make your name great, and you will be a blessing. And I will bless you, and make your name great; and so you shall be a blessing" (Genesis 12:2-3). If we are blessed with resources beyond our needs, it is not for the purpose of living more lavishly but to bless others. We are blessed to be a blessing.

BE WILLING TO SHARE
"Command them [the rich] to do good, to be rich in good deeds, and to be generous and willing to share" (I Timothy 6:18).

GIVE TO BREAK THE HOLD OF MONEY
Another reason to give is that doing so breaks the hold that money might otherwise have on us. While the Bible doesn't specifically say so, it is evident that persons who give freely and generously are not controlled by money but have freedom.

GIVE JOYFULLY, GENEROUSLY, IN A TIMELY MANNER
"Out of the most severe trial, their overflowing joy and their extreme poverty welled up in rich generosity. For I testify that they gave as much as they were able, and even beyond their ability. Entirely on their own, they urgently pleaded with us for the privilege of sharing in this service to the saints" (2 Corinthians 8:1-5).

GIVE WISELY
"We want to avoid any criticism of the way we administer this liberal gift" (2 Corinthians 8:20).

GIVE EXPECTANTLY AND CHEERFULLY
"The one who plants generously will get a generous crop. You must each make up your own mind as to how much you should give. Don't give reluctantly or in response to pressure. For God loves the person who gives cheerfully" (2 Corinthians 9:6-7 NLT; see also verses 10-14).

MOTIVES FOR GIVING ARE IMPORTANT

Unless our motives are right, we can give all we have—even our bodies as sacrifices—and it will be for naught (I Corinthians 13). We can be scrupulous with tithing and still not have the right motives. Jesus rebuked the religious leaders of his day for this very thing: "You hypocrites! You give a tenth of your spices—mint, dill and cummin. But you have neglected the more important matters of the law—justice, mercy and faithfulness" (Matthew 23:23).

SAVING

The Wise Saver—One who builds, preserves, and invests with discernment.

IT IS WISE TO SAVE

"In the house of the wise are stores of choice food and oil, but [the] foolish . . . devour all [they have]" (Proverbs 21:20). "Go to the ant, you sluggard; consider its ways and be wise! It has no commander, no overseer or ruler, yet it stores its provisions in summer and gathers it food at harvest" (Proverbs 6:8).

IT IS SINFUL TO HOARD

And he gave them an illustration: "A rich man had a fertile farm that produced fine crops. In fact, his barns were full to overflowing. So he said, 'I know! I'll tear down my barns and build bigger ones. Then I'll have room enough to store everything. And I'll sit back and say to myself, My friend, you have enough stored away for years to come. Now take it easy! Eat, drink, and be merry!' But God said to him, 'You fool! You will die this very night. Then who will get it all?' Yes, a person is a fool to store up earthly wealth but not have a rich relationship with God" (Luke 12:16–21 NLT).

CALCULATE COST; PRIORITIZE

"But don't begin until you count the cost. For who would begin construction of a building without first getting estimates and then checking to see if there is enough money to pay the bills? Otherwise, you might complete only the foundation before running out of funds. And then how everyone would laugh at you! They would say, 'There's the person who started that building and ran out of money before it was finished!'" (Luke 14:28–30 NLT).

AVOID GET-RICH-QUICK SCHEMES

"The trustworthy will get a rich reward. But the person who wants to get rich quick will only get into trouble" (Proverbs 28:20 NLT).

SEEK WISE COUNSELORS

"Let the wise listen and add to their learning, and let the discerning get guidance" (Proverbs 1:5).

ESTABLISH A JOB BEFORE BUYING HOME

"Finish your outdoor work and get your fields ready; after that, build your house" (Proverbs 24:27).

DIVERSIFY YOUR HOLDINGS

"Give portions to seven, yes to eight, for you do not know what disaster will come upon the land" (Ecclesiastes 11:2).

DEBT

The Cautious Debtor—One who avoids entering into debt, is careful and strategic when incurring debt, and always repays debt.

REPAY DEBT AND DO SO PROMPTLY

"The wicked borrow and do not repay, but the righteous give generously" (Psalm 37:21). " Do not say to your neighbor, 'Come back later; I'll give it tomorrow'—when you now have it with you" (Proverbs 3:28).

AVOID THE BONDAGE OF DEBT

"The rich rule over the poor, and the borrower is servant to the lender" (Proverbs 22:7).

DEBT PRESUMES ON THE FUTURE

"Now listen, you who say, 'Today or tomorrow we will go to this or that city, spend a year there, carry on business and make money.' Why, you do not even know what will happen tomorrow. What is your life? You are a mist that appears for a little while and then vanishes" (James 4:13–14).

DEBT CAN DENY GOD THE OPPORTUNITY TO WORK IN OUR LIVES AND TEACH US VALUABLE LESSONS

God may wish to show us his love by providing us with something we desire but for which we have no resources. If we go into debt to get it anyway, we deny him that opportunity (see Luke 12:22–32). In the same way that parents refrain from giving a child everything the child wants because parents know it isn't in the child's best interest, incurring debt can rob God of the opportunity to teach us through denial. Ecclesiastes 7:14 reminds us: "When times are good, be happy; but when times are bad, consider: God has made the one as well as the other."

DEBT CAN FOSTER ENVY AND GREED

"Beware! Don't be greedy for what you don't have. Real life is not measured by how much we own" (Luke 12:15).

GIVE AND PAY WHAT YOU OWE

"Give everyone what you owe them: Pay your taxes and import duties, and give respect and honor to all to whom it is due" (Romans 13:7 NLT).

DON'T CO-SIGN

"Do not co-sign another person's note or put up a guarantee for someone else's loan. If you can't pay it, even your bed will be snatched from under you" (Proverbs 22:26–27 NLT).

DEBT CAN DISRUPT SPIRITUAL GROWTH

"The fruit of the Spirit is love, joy, peace, patience, kindness, goodness, faithfulness, gentleness and self-control. Against such things there is no law" (Galatians 5:22-23).

SPENDING

The Prudent Consumer—One who enjoys the fruits of their labor yet guards against materialism.

BEWARE OF IDOLS

"You shall not make yourself an idol in the form of anything in heaven above or on the earth beneath or in the waters below" (Deuteronomy 5:8). Materialism—which so saturates our culture—is nothing less than a competing theology in which matter (things) is of ultimate significance; that is, things become gods or idols. "They . . . worshipped and served created things rather than the Creator" (Romans 1:25).

GUARD AGAINST GREED; THINGS DO NOT BRING HAPPINESS

"Beware! Don't be greedy for what you don't have. Real life is not measured by how much we own" (Luke 12:15).

SEEK MODERATION

"Give me neither poverty nor riches, but give me only my daily bread. Otherwise, I may have too much and disown you and say, 'Who is the LORD?' Or I may become poor and steal, and so dishonor the name of my God" (Proverbs 30:8-9).

BE CONTENT

"I know what it is to be in need, and I know what it is to have plenty. I have learned the secret of being content in any and every situation, whether well fed or hungry, whether living in plenty or in want. I can do everything through him who gives me strength" (Philippians 4:12–13).

"Godliness with contentment is great gain. For we brought nothing into the world, and we can take nothing out of it. But if we have food and clothing, we will be content with that" (1 Timothy 6:6–8).

DON'T WASTE GOD'S RESOURCES

"When they had all had enough to eat, he said to his disciples, 'Gather the pieces that are left over. Let nothing be wasted'" (John 6:12).

ENJOY A PORTION OF GOD'S PROVISION

"Command those who are rich in this present world not to be arrogant nor to put their hope in wealth, which is so uncertain, but to put their hope in God, who richly provides us with everything for our enjoyment. Command them to do good, to be rich in good deeds, and to be generous and willing to share. In this way they will lay up treasure for themselves as a firm foundation for the coming age, so that they may take hold of the life that is truly life" (1 Timothy 6:17–19).

WATCH YOUR FINANCES (BUDGET)

"Be sure you know the condition of your flocks, give careful attention to your herds; for riches do not endure forever, and a crown is not secure for all generations" (Proverbs 27:23–24).

SPENDING PLAN

EARNINGS/INCOME PER MONTH	TOTALS
Salary #1 (net take-home)	_____
Salary #2 (net take-home)	_____
Other (less taxes)	_____
TOTAL MONTHLY INCOME	$_____

% GUIDE

1. GIVING $_____

- Church _____
- OTHER CONTRIBUTIONS _____

2. SAVING   5–10% $_____

- EMERGENCY _____
- REPLACEMENT _____
- LONG TERM _____

3. DEBT   0–10% $_____

- CREDIT CARDS:
  - VISA _____
  - Master Card _____
  - Discover _____
  - American Express _____
  - Gas Cards _____
  - Department Stores _____
- EDUCATION LOANS _____
- OTHER LOANS:
  - Bank Loans _____
  - Credit Union _____
  - Family/Friends _____
  - OTHER _____

4. HOUSING   25–38% $_____

- MORTGAGE/TAXES/RENT _____
- MAINTENANCE/REPAIRS _____
- UTILITIES:
  - Electric _____
  - Gas _____
  - Water _____
  - Trash _____
  - Telephone/Internet _____
  - Cable TV _____
  - OTHER _____

5. AUTO/TRANSP.   12–15% $_____

- CAR PAYMENTS/LICENSE _____
- GAS & BUS/TRAIN/PARKING _____
- OIL/LUBE/MAINTENANCE _____

---

* This is a % of total monthly income. These are guidelines only and may be different for individual situations. However, there should be good rationale for a significant variance.

6. INSURANCE
(Paid by you)   5% $_____

- AUTO _____
- HOMEOWNERS _____
- LIFE _____
- MEDICAL/DENTAL _____
- Other _____

7. HOUSEHOLD/PERSONAL   15–25% $_____

- GROCERIES _____
- CLOTHES/DRY CLEANING _____
- GIFTS _____
- HOUSEHOLD ITEMS _____
- PERSONAL:
  - Liquor/Tobacco _____
  - Cosmetics _____
  - Barber/Beauty _____
- OTHER:
  - Books/Magazines _____
  - Allowances _____
  - Music Lessons _____
  - Personal Technology _____
  - Education _____
  - Miscellaneous _____

8. ENTERTAINMENT   5–10% $_____

- GOING OUT:
  - Meals _____
  - Movies/Events _____
  - Baby-sitting _____
- TRAVEL (VACATION/TRIPS) _____
- OTHER:
  - Fitness/Sports _____
  - Hobbies _____
  - Media Rental _____
  - OTHER _____

9. PROF. SERVICES   5–15% $_____

- CHILD CARE _____
- MEDICAL/DENTAL/PRESC. _____
- OTHER
  - Legal _____
  - Counseling _____
  - Professional Dues _____

10. MISC. SMALL CASH EXPENDITURES   2–3% $_____

TOTAL EXPENSES $_____

TOTAL MONTHLY INCOME	$_____
LESS TOTAL EXPENSES	$_____
INCOME OVER/(UNDER) EXPENSES	$_____

Spending Record

Daily Variable Expenses

	Transportation		Household						Professional Services	Entertainment		
	Gas, etc.	Maint/ Repair	Groceries	Clothes	Gifts	Household Items	Personal	Other		Going Out	Travel	Other
(1) Spending Plan												
1												
2												
3												
4												
5												
6												
7												
8												
9												
10												
11												
12												
13												
14												
15												
16												
17												
18												
19												
20												
21												
22												
23												
24												
25												
26												
27												
28												
29												
30												
31												
(2) Total												
(3) (Over)/Under												
(4) Last Month YTD												
(5) Total Year—to—Date												

- Use this page to record expenses that tend to be daily, variable expenses—often the hardest to control.
- Keep receipts throughout the day and record them at the end of the day.
- Total each category at the end of the month (line 2) and compare to the Spending Plan (line 1). Subtracting line 2 from line 1 gives you an (over) or under the budget figure for that month (line 3).
- To verify that you have made each day's entry, cross out the number at the bottom of the page that corresponds to that day's date.
- Optional: If you wish to monitor your progress as you go through the year, you can keep cumulative totals in lines 4 and 5.

Spending Record

Month _____

Monthly Regular Expenses
(generally paid by check once a month)

	Giving		Savings	Debt			Housing				Auto	Insurance		Misc. Cash Exp.
	Church	Other		Credit Cards	Educ.	Other	Mort./Rent	Maint.	Util.	Other	Pmts.	Auto/Home	Life/Med.	
(1) Spending Plan														
(2) Total														
(3) (Over)/Under														
(4) Last Mo. YTD														
(5) This Mo. YTD														

- This page allows you to record major monthly expenses for which you typically write just one or two checks per month.
- Entries can be recorded as the checks are written (preferably) or by referring back to the check ledger at a convenient time.
- Total each category at the end of the month (line 2) and compare to the Spending Plan (line 1). Subtracting line 2 from line 1 gives you an (over) or under the budget figure for that month (line 3).
- Use the "Monthly Assessment" section to reflect on the future actions that will be helpful in staying on course.

Monthly Assessment

Area	(Over)/Under	Reason	Future Action

Areas of Victory _____

Areas to Watch _____

Spending Record

Month _____

	Daily Variable Expenses											
	Transportation		Household						Professional Services	Entertainment		
	Gas, etc.	Maint/ Repair	Groceries	Clothes	Gifts	Household Items	Personal	Other		Going Out	Travel	Other
(1) Spending Plan												
1												
2												
3												
4												
5												
6												
7												
8												
9												
10												
11												
12												
13												
14												
15												
16												
17												
18												
19												
20												
21												
22												
23												
24												
25												
26												
27												
28												
29												
30												
31												
(2) Total												
(3) (Over)/Under												
(4) Last Month YTD												
(5) Total Year–to–Date												

- Use this page to record expenses that tend to be daily, variable expenses—often the hardest to control.
- Keep receipts throughout the day and record them at the end of the day.
- Total each category at the end of the month (line 2) and compare to the Spending Plan (line 1). Subtracting line 2 from line 1 gives you an (over) or under the budget figure for that month (line 3).
- To verify that you have made each day's entry, cross out the number at the bottom of the page that corresponds to that day's date.
- Optional: If you wish to monitor your progress as you go through the year, you can keep cumulative totals in lines 4 and 5.

149

Spending Record

Month _____

Monthly Regular Expenses
(generally paid by check once a month)

	Giving		Savings	Debt			Housing				Auto	Insurance		Misc. Cash Exp.
	Church	Other		Credit Cards	Educ.	Other	Mort./Rent	Maint.	Util.	Other	Pmts.	Auto/Home	Life/Med.	
(1) Spending Plan														
(2) Total														
(3) (Over)/Under														
(4) Last Mo. YTD														
(5) This Mo. YTD														

- This page allows you to record major monthly expenses for which you typically write just one or two checks per month.
- Entries can be recorded as the checks are written (preferably) or by referring back to the check ledger at a convenient time.
- Total each category at the end of the month (line 2) and compare to the Spending Plan (line 1). Subtracting line 2 from line 1 gives you an (over) or under the budget figure for that month (line 3).
- Use the "Monthly Assessment" section to reflect on the future actions that will be helpful in staying on course.

Monthly Assessment

Area	(Over)/Under	Reason	Future Action

Areas of Victory _____

Areas to Watch _____

Month _____

Spending Record

	Daily Variable Expenses												
	Transportation		Household						Professional Services	Entertainment			
	Gas, etc.	Maint/ Repair	Groceries	Clothes	Gifts	Household Items	Personal	Other		Going Out	Travel	Other	
(1) Spending Plan													
(2) Total													
(3) (Over)/Under													
(4) Last Month YTD													
(5) Total Year-to-Date													

1	2	3	4	5	6	7	8	9	10	11	12	13	14	15	16	17	18	19	20	21	22	23	24	25	26	27	28	29	30	31

- Use this page to record expenses that tend to be daily, variable expenses—often the hardest to control.
- Keep receipts throughout the day and record them at the end of the day.
- Total each category at the end of the month (line 2) and compare to the Spending Plan (line 1). Subtracting line 2 from line 1 gives you an (over) or under the budget figure for that month (line 3).
- To verify that you have made each day's entry, cross out the number at the bottom of the page that corresponds to that day's date.
- Optional: If you wish to monitor your progress as you go through the year, you can keep cumulative totals in lines 4 and 5.

Spending Record

Month _____

Monthly Regular Expenses
(generally paid by check once a month)

	Giving		Savings	Debt				Housing				Auto	Insurance		Misc. Cash Exp.
	Church	Other		Credit Cards	Educ.	Other	Mort./Rent	Maint.	Util.	Other		Pmts.	Auto/Home	Life/Med.	
(1) Spending Plan															
(2) Total															
(3) (Over)/Under															
(4) Last Mo. YTD															
(5) This Mo. YTD															

- This page allows you to record major monthly expenses for which you typically write just one or two checks per month.
- Entries can be recorded as the checks are written (preferably) or by referring back to the check ledger at a convenient time.
- Total each category at the end of the month (line 2) and compare to the Spending Plan (line 1). Subtracting line 2 from line 1 gives you an (over) or under the budget figure for that month (line 3).
- Use the "Monthly Assessment" section to reflect on the future actions that will be helpful in staying on course.

Monthly Assessment

Area	(Over)/Under	Reason	Future Action

Areas of Victory _____

Areas to Watch _____

152

NOTES

NOTES

NOTES

NOTES

WILLOW CREEK ASSOCIATION

Vision,   Training,   Resources

for Prevailing Churches

This resource was created to serve you and to help you in building a local church that prevails!

Since 1992, the Willow Creek Association (WCA) has been linking like-minded, action-oriented churches with each other and with strategic vision, training, and resources. Now a worldwide network of over 7,000 churches from more than ninety denominations, the WCA works to equip Member Churches and others with the tools needed to build prevailing churches. Our desire is to inspire, equip, and encourage Christian leaders to build biblically functioning "Acts 2" churches that reach increasing numbers of unchurched people, not just with innovations from Willow Creek Community Church in South Barrington, Illinois, but from any church in the world that has experienced God-given breakthroughs.

Willow Creek Conferences

Each year, thousands of local church leaders, staff and volunteers—from WCA Member Churches and others—attend one of our conferences or training events. Conferences offered on the Willow Creek campus in South Barrington, Illinois, include:

- Prevailing Church Conference—Offered twice a year, it is the foundational, overarching, training conference for staff and volunteers working to build a prevailing local church.
- Select ministry workshops—A wide variety of strategic, day-long workshops covering seven topic areas that represent key characteristics of a prevailing church; offered multiple times throughout the year.
- Promiseland Conference—Children's ministries; infant through fifth grade.
- Student Ministries Conference—Junior and senior high ministries.
- Arts Conference—Vision and training for Christian artists using their gifts in the ministries of local churches.
- Leadership Summit—Envisioning and equipping Christians with leadership gifts and responsibilities; broadcast live via satellite to scores of cities across North America.
- Contagious Evangelism Conference—Encouragement and training for churches and church leaders who want to be strategic in reaching lost people for Christ.
- Small Groups Conference—Exploring how developing a church of small groups can play a vital role in developing authentic Christian community that leads to spiritual transformation.

To find out more about WCA conferences, visit our website at www.willowcreek.com.

Regional Conferences and Training Events

Each year the WCA team leads a variety of topical conferences and training events in select cities across the United States. Ministry and topic topic areas include leadership, next-generation ministries, small groups, arts and worship, evangelism, spiritual gifts, financial stewardship, and spiritual formation. These events make quality training more accessible and affordable to larger groups of staff and volunteers.

To find out more about upcoming events in your area, visit our website at www.willowcreek.com.

Willow Creek Resources®

Churches can look to Willow Creek Resources® for a trusted channel of ministry tools in areas of leadership, evangelism, spiritual gifts, small groups, drama, contemporary music, financial stewardship, spiritual transformation, and more. For ordering information, call (800) 570-9812 or visit our website at www.willowcreek.com.

WCA Membership

Membership in the Willow Creek Association as well as attendance at WCA Conferences is for churches, ministries, and leaders who hold to an historic, orthodox understanding of biblical Christianity. The annual church membership fee of $249 provides substantial discounts for your entire team on all conferences and Willow Creek Resources, networking opportunities with other outreach-oriented churches, a bimonthly newsletter, a subscription to the Defining Moments monthly audio journal for leaders, and more.

To find out more about WCA membership, visit our website at www.willowcreek.com.

WillowNet www.willowcreek.com

This Internet resource service provides access to hundreds of Willow Creek messages, drama scripts, songs, videos, and multimedia ideas. The system allows you to sort through these elements and download them for a fee.

Our website also provides detailed information on the Willow Creek Association, Willow Creek Community Church, WCA membership, conferences, training events, resources, and more.

WillowCharts.com www.WillowCharts.com

Designed for local church worship leaders and musicians, WillowCharts.com provides online access to hundreds of music charts and chart components, including choir, orchestral, and horn sections, as well as rehearsal tracks and video streaming of Willow Creek Community Church performances.

The NET http://studentministry.willowcreek.com

The NET is an online training and resource center designed by and for student ministry leaders. It provides an inside look at the structure, vision, and mission of prevailing student ministries from around the world. The NET gives leaders access to complete programming elements, including message outlines, dramas, small group questions, and more. An indispensable resource and networking tool for prevailing student ministry leaders!

Contact the Willow Creek Association

If you have comments or questions, or would like to find out more about WCA events or resources, please contact us:

Willow Creek Association
P.O. Box 3188
Barrington, IL 60011-3188
Phone: (800) 570-9812 or (847) 765-0070
Fax (888) 922-0035 or (847) 765-5046
Web: www.willowcreek.com